Physical Charac
Flat-Coate

(from the American Ken

Topline: Strong and level.

Loin: Strong, well muscled and long enough to allow fo ement and length of stride.

Coat: Of moderate length, density and with a high luster. The ideal coat is straight ng.

Tail: Fairly straight, well set on, with bone reaching approximately to the hock joint.

Size: Preferred height is 23 to 24.5 inches at the withers for dogs, 22 to 23.5 inches for bitches.

Hindquarters: Powerful with angulation in balance with the front assembly. Upper thighs powerful and well muscled. Good turn of stifle with sound, strong joint. Hock joint strong, well let down.

Feet: Oval or round. Medium sized and tight with well arched toes and thick pads.

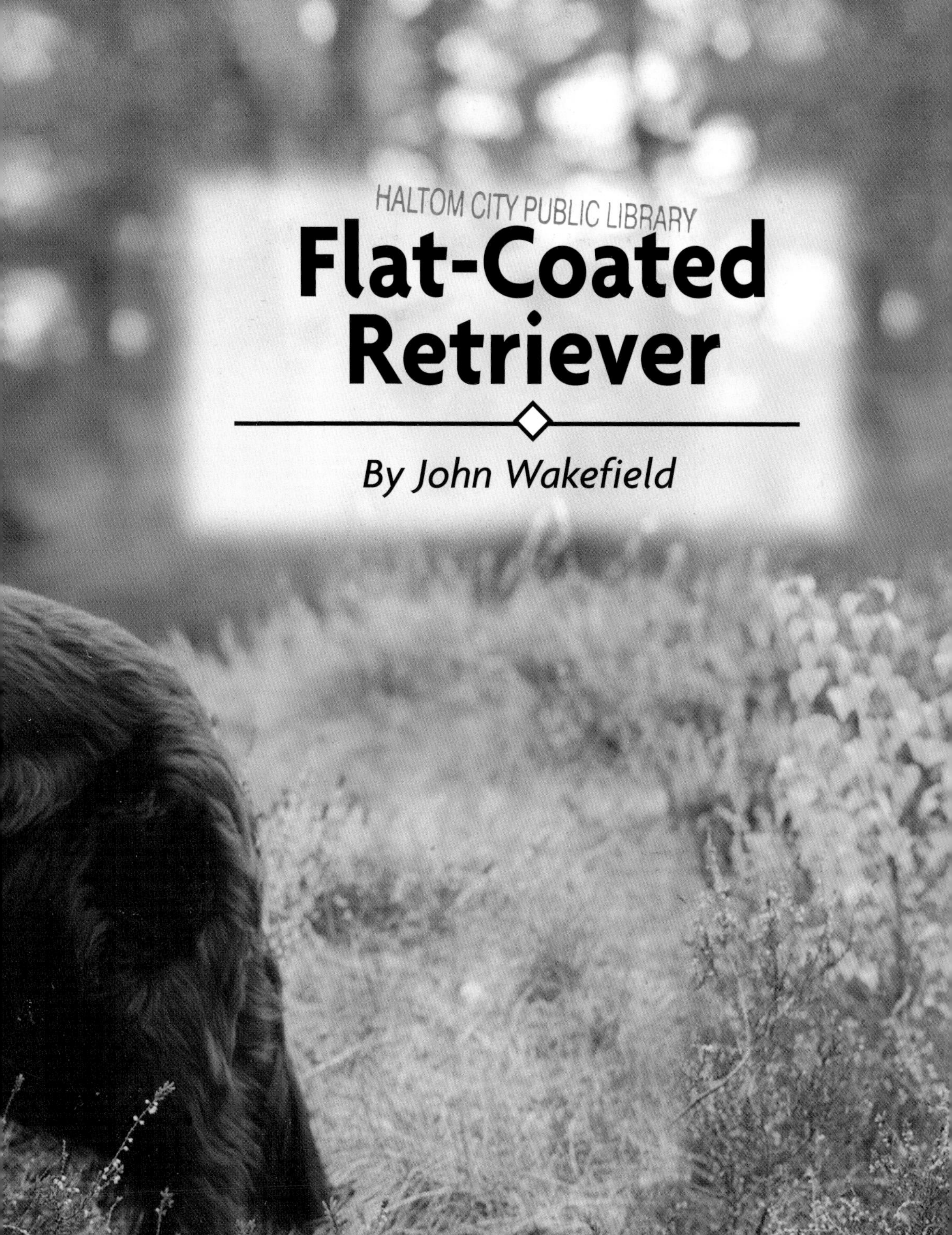

Flat-Coated Retriever

By John Wakefield

Contents

9 **History of the** Flat-Coated Retriever

Known from its beginnings as a superior worker who possessed form as well as function, the Flat-Coated Retriever has always been a favorite in the field and in the show ring. Follow the evolution of the breed and learn about the people who were instrumental in its establishment.

18 **Characteristics of the** Flat-Coated Retriever

Energetic, puppy-like and gregarious, the Flat-Coated Retriever is always ready for action and to make a new friend. Discover the unique traits that distinguish the Flat-Coat from the other retriever breeds; also learn about its physical characteristics and breed-specific abilities.

24 **Breed Standard for the** Flat-Coated Retriever

Learn the requirements of a well-bred Flat-Coated Retriever by studying the description of the breed set forth in the American Kennel Club standard. Both show dogs and pets must possess key characteristics as outlined in the breed standard.

30 **Your Puppy** Flat-Coated Retriever

Find out about how to locate a well-bred Flat-Coated Retriever puppy. Discover which questions to ask the breeder and what to expect when visiting the litter. Prepare for your puppy-accessory shopping spree. Also discussed are home safety, the first trip to the vet, socialization and some basic puppy problems.

57 **Proper Care of Your** Flat-Coated Retriever

Cover the specifics of taking care of your Flat-Coated Retriever every day: feeding for the puppy, adult and senior dog; grooming, including coat care, ears, eyes, nails and bathing; and exercise needs for your dog. Also discussed are dog ID and boarding.

Training Your Flat-Coated Retriever 72

Begin with the basics of training the puppy and adult dog. Learn the principles of house-training the Flat-Coated Retriever, including the use of crates and basic scent instincts. Get started by introducing the pup to his collar and leash, and progress to the basic commands. Find out about obedience classes and other activities.

Healthcare of Your Flat-Coated Retriever 99

By Lowell Ackerman DVM, DACVD
Become your dog's healthcare advocate and a well-educated canine keeper. Select a skilled and able veterinarian. Discuss pet insurance, vaccinations and infectious diseases, the neuter/spay decision, parasite control and breed-specific health concerns, along with a special section on canine eye disease.

Your Senior Flat-Coated Retriever 139

Know when to consider your Flat-Coated Retriever a senior and what special needs he will have. Learn to recognize the signs of aging in terms of physical and behavioral traits and what your vet can do to optimize your dog's golden years. Consider some advice about saying goodbye to your beloved pet.

Showing Your Flat-Coated Retriever 147

Step into the center ring and find out about the world of showing pure-bred dogs. Here's how to get started in AKC shows, how they are organized and what's required for your dog to become a champion. Take a leap into the realms of obedience trials, agility, tracking tests, field trials and hunting events.

Index 156

KENNEL CLUB BOOKS: **FLAT-COATED RETRIEVER**

ISBN: 1-59378-220-9

308 Main Street, Allenhurst, NJ 07711 USA

Cover Design Patented: US 6,435,559 B2 • Printed in South Korea

10 9 8 7 6 5 4 3 2 1

Photography by Carol Ann Johnson and Alice Roche
with additional photographs by

Paulette Braun, T.J. Calhoun, Carolina Biological Supply, Isabelle Français, Bill Jonas, Dr. Dennis Kunkel, Tam C. Nguyen, Phototake, Jean Claude Revy and Alice van Kempen.

Illustrations by Renée Low and Patricia Peters.

The publisher wishes to thank all of the owners of the dogs featured in this book, including Gillian Impey, Sean McGrath and Margaret Palven.

HISTORY OF THE

FLAT-COATED RETRIEVER

Throughout history, the pairing of the hunter and the hunting dog has evolved according to whatever hunting conditions existed at the time. Prior to the 1800s, the primitive weaponry dictated the type of canine used to locate and pursue game birds and other animals. The introduction of the shotgun changed forever the nature of the human-canine hunting partnership.

With his improved weaponry offering greater distance and advantage in downing large numbers of upland game and waterfowl, the hunter also needed an improved retrieving dog to locate, collect and deliver those shot birds to hand. Use of the shotgun demanded a controllable dog that would locate game within gun range.

The Flat-Coated Retriever has always been an all-around favorite—loved for its ability in the field, its beauty and its temperament.

During that period, the name "retriever" was used to define the function of any general-purpose hunting dog, rather than to refer to a specific breed of dog. Thus any pointer, spaniel or setter that also retrieved the game shot by its hunting master was considered a retriever. Sportsmen and market hunters used a variety of such hunting dogs to pursue their sport and

NO YELLOW ALLOWED

Yellow is a disqualifying color in the Flat-Coated Retriever. Many long-time breeders who believe that health problems automatically accompany the color are adamant about keeping yellow out and will insist a yellow Flat-Coated Retriever be spayed or neutered. While the yellow color is rare, it is not valuable and should not command a higher price.

livelihood, and most dog breedings were planned and accomplished according to the game-finding ability of individual dogs. They simply bred good hunting dogs of any origin to other accomplished dogs in order to produce superior hunting dogs with certain qualities such as scenting ability, courage or water affinity, rather than promote a particular type or breed.

Due to this random selection process and the lack of breeding records, the exact sequence of the development of the retriever breeds is lost in the mist of history. Thus confusion reigns over the exact origin of most retriever breeds. The exception is the Golden Retriever, which was developed by a single individual whose breeding efforts were locked into canine history by his kennel records.

Around 1850, as various retriever types were evolving and developing in England, the St. John's Water Dog from Labrador emerged as an outstanding retrieving dog that possessed exceptional intelligence, stamina and good health. It is commonly believed that crosses to these dogs from Labrador resulted in the establishment of the Labrador Retriever, Curly-Coated Retriever and Wavy-Coated Retriever, which later became the Flat-Coated Retriever.

The Wavy-Coated Retriever became known as a superb working dog that combined working ability with grace and beauty. Such elegance was not lost on those sportsmen who also fancied comely dogs, and within two decades the athletic, racy Flat-Coat type had been "fixed," producing a dual-purpose dog that performed in the field and had potential in the show ring.

This famous photo from the 1930s shows Fanny, belonging to Mr. J. Smart, carrying his master's pet ferret. Neither of these family pets seems to mind this unusual method of transport.

The first Flat-Coated Retrievers were exhibited in 1864 in two classes at a show in Birmingham, England. The winners were Mr. T. Meyrick's Wyndham and Lord Paget's Music, the first two Flat-Coats to launch the breed's ascent in both venues of canine competition.

By the early 1870s, the versatile Flat-Coat had caught the eye of Mr. Sewallis Evelyn Shirley, a prominent breeder and fancier who bred outstanding dual-purpose dogs under the Ettington prefix.

Mr. Shirley was perhaps best known as the founder of England's Kennel Club in 1873, where he also served as its first president and chairman. His experience and association with The Kennel Club assured the breed of dual-purpose quality in showing on the bench as well as working ability in the field.

It is thought that Mr. Shirley used the St. John's Water Dogs, water spaniels and possibly Scotch collies to stabilize and fix the type of the Flat-Coat breed.

Stainton Spinner was a Flat-Coated Retriever owned by Mr. T. H. Moorby. This type of dog was advertised as being both a field and bench dog.

He also used the Labrador Retriever in some breedings, using available dogs from two major English Labrador kennels, Malmesbury and Buccleuch. Mr. Shirley's Flat-Coats were primarily black or liver, although other colors were considered acceptable at that time. During that period, Flat-Coats were still referred to as Wavy-Coated Retrievers.

The great Betty of Riverside is a beautiful example of H. Reginald Cooke's Riverside strain of Flat-Coats. Mr. Cooke was one of the leading breeders and breed authorities of his time.

COLOR GENETICS

The liver color is recessive to black, which means both parents of a liver Flat-Coated Retriever must carry at least one gene for that color, even if both parents are black.

A liver Flat-Coated Retriever carries only liver genes, and two livers can produce only the liver color, never black.

Two other prominent breeders of the late 1800s succeeded Mr. Shirley in his dedication to setting and preserving type in Flat-Coated Retrievers. Mr. Harding Cox followed Mr. Shirley's example and produced Flat-Coats that were well known for their elegant heads and similarity of type. Another patron of the breed, Colonel Cornwall-Leigh, also was known for considerable contributions to the breed.

Mr. H. Reginald Cooke (1850–1951), was an influential fancier who was well known by his Riverside prefix. He kept Flat-Coats for over 60 years and is regarded as the most notable patron of the breed. Concerned with preserving the hunting ability in the show dog, Mr. Cooke was successful in field trials as well as the show ring, and his efforts helped the breed retain its dual-purpose nature. The spectacular Riverside kennel has produced great numbers of top-winning show and field dogs, with statistics that rival any kennel in any breed.

Mr. Cooke was a keen competitor, determined to breed and campaign the best-quality dogs possible. He was a formidable handler and exhibitor, and during his career his field trial record included 15 first placements, 10 seconds, 11 Reserves and 21 Certificates of Merit. He also won 349 Challenge Certificates (CCs, the

Mrs. Phizacklea with four of her famed Atherbram Flat-Coated Retrievers, all of which were prize-winning dogs.

Probably the most famous painting of a Flat-Coated Retriever is this rendition of the well-known Eng. Ch. High Leigh Blarney, owned by Colonel Cornwall-Leigh and then H. Reginald Cooke, both prominent in the breed. The painting was executed by Maud Earl, an outstanding painter of dogs.

building blocks of British championships) and 130 Reserve CCs, and made up many champions, including Toby of Riverside and Grouse of Riverside, who both became dual champions.

Mr. Cooke kept detailed breeding records, which are preserved today as part of Flat-Coat history. Passionate about promoting the best in the breed, he also wrote three small brochures to help educate the novice about the breed.

Mr. Cooke's, Mr. Cox's and Colonel Cornwall-Leigh's dedication to the Flat-Coat helped to establish the breed as a favored choice of pure-bred dog. By the late 1800s, the Flat-Coat was recognized for its beauty and ability as well as for being a breed well fixed in character and quality. Known especially for their graceful movement, sleek good looks and pleasing expressions, Flat-Coats became favorites in both field trials and the show ring.

Colonel Cornwall-Leigh's High Leigh Blarney was a leading contender during his career. When the Colonel passed away in 1905, his dogs were put up at auction. Mr. Cooke was so greatly impressed with Blarney that he moved forward to purchase him. Mr. Cooke's agent successfully secured the dog for

The old type of Flat-Coated Retriever, as shown here, was thought by some to be too heavy for hunting and retrieving.

200 guineas. That was a grand price in those days, but Mr. Cooke easily recovered his investment in stud fees in just two years.

Blarney continued his winning ways and remained unbeaten in the show ring until his death at 11 years of age. Used frequently at stud for his superb qualities, he left a lasting imprint on the breed.

Mr. Cooke's success with Blarney no doubt influenced his future plans, and he went on to pay 200 guineas for Eng. Ch. Black Quilt. Lord Redesdale followed suit and purchased a bitch, Eng. Ch. Black Queen, for 145 guineas. Although the Flat-Coated Retriever was apparently in demand given those steep purchases, the smaller kennels and less wealthy fanciers were unable to compete due to those inflated prices demanded by the larger and more influential breeders of the day.

At the end of the 19th century the Flat-Coat was the top retriever in England and his popularity had spread across the Atlantic to the US, with AKC registration in 1915. However, several factors were about to influence the breed negatively in both countries. First, around this same time, the Labrador and Golden Retrievers were on the rise, with both breeds growing in numbers and popularity in the UK and the US. These breeds soon surpassed the Flat-Coat, which was typically

Kennett Ruth, owned by Major H. L. A. Swann, retrieves game that fell on the wrong side of the road. Roads often caused a bother to the shooters, as people would gather to sightsee.

bred in smaller numbers and kept by English gamekeepers rather than bred in larger kennels. Nonetheless, the real decline in Flat-Coat numbers was caused by the two World Wars, which had negative effects on all breeds of pure-bred dog, as much breeding activity dwindled or ceased completely.

By the time World War II had ended, the influence of the war years and the popularity of the Labrador and Golden Retrievers had trampled the Flat-Coat's popularity. The breed reappeared in England in 1946 at an Open Show in Leeds. The Flat-Coat's preservation and re-establishment in England is credited to the efforts of several dedicated breeders in the post-war years, one of these being Mr. and Mrs. W. J. Phizacklea, whose Atherbram line produced strong dual-purpose dogs in both liver and black. His breeding program produced the majority of Flat-Coats in England following World War II.

Another notable English breeder whose dedication truly helped to save the breed is Mr. Stanley O'Neill of the Pewcroft Kennel. Mr. O'Neill put much research and study into his breeding, sharing his advice and knowledge with other breeders, fanciers and owners. He produced three litters that would become foundation stock for other kennels in the UK, and was instrumental in the revival of the breed in the US, with his Pewcroft Prefect being among the first post-war exports to the US.

A COAT FOR ALL SEASONS

The Flat-Coated Retriever is a double-coated breed, possessing an outer coat of long silky guard hairs and a soft downy undercoat that insulates the dog from temperature extremes. This is an important characteristic in a dog that must retrieve birds, especially waterfowl, under all weather conditions.

Homer Downing was a major force in the breed in the US at that time, being the recipient of Pewcroft Prefect in 1953. Called "Doc," this dog became the first dog to earn the UDT title in the Flat-Coat breed. UDT stands for Utility Dog Tracker, meaning that the dog has earned titles at high levels of both obedience and tracking competition. Mr. Downing then in 1955 imported

Another of H. Reginald Cooke's famous dogs, Ch. Worsley Bess, memorialized in a lovely painting by Maud Earl.

the bitch Atherbram Stella who, two years later, gave birth to the first American-born litter in a decade. A mating of Doc and Stella produced one of the most notable Flat-Coats of his day, Ch. Bramcroft Dandy, UD, owned by Sally Terroux, who also owned some significant UK imports. He was highly successful in the breed ring, winning almost all of the shows that he entered. This dog was a multiple breed winner, multiple Group winner and highly successful obedience dog.

From the mid-1950s on, the breed was on firm footing but numbers were low. A sudden surge occurred in the late 1960s and beginning of the 1970s, with a marked increase in registrations and members of the breed entered, and earning titles, in the conformation and obedience rings. Today, the Flat-Coat hovers around the 100th-place mark in terms of popularity as measured by AKC registration statistics, with well over 500 Flat-Coats being registered annually. Of course, these numbers don't begin to compare to the sky-high registration statistics of the Golden and Labrador Retrievers but, then again, the Flat-Coated Retriever is in a class by himself!

The one definitive feature that sets the Flat-Coat apart from other retriever breeds, and continues to distinguish it from all other breeds, is the breeders' dedication

Busy Mite, owned by E. W. H. Blagg, is a perfect example of what Flat-Coats looked like in the early 1900s.

FCRSA

The Flat-Coated Retriever Society of America (FCRSA) was formed in 1960. Membership has increased greatly since the club's inception, from 15 members to over 800! Two prestigious awards offered by the club are given in honor of the achievements of the well-known Doc and his equally notable owner, Homer Downing: the Bramcroft Obedience Trophy, established in 1972, and the Field Trial Trophy, established in 1975. These two awards are certainly a testament to the club's commitment to preserving the dual-purpose, all-around abilities of the Flat-Coated Retriever breed.

to preserving and promoting Flat-Coat working ability. Unlike the other retriever breeds, the Flat-Coat has not yet split into two different types, bred for either the show ring or ability in the field. The Flat-Coated Retriever should be a tireless, willing and biddable worker that excels in locating fallen game. Only the relentless efforts of those who love the breed will maintain its versatility as a retriever that enjoys and excels at working disciplines in the field, tracking, obedience, agility and flyball. It is important to note that most Flat-Coats shown in conformation were, and still are today, worked in the field or in performance events.

Flat-Coated Retrievers are as comfortable in the water as they are on land, thanks to their insulating coats.

CHARACTERISTICS OF THE

FLAT-COATED RETRIEVER

BE GENTLE AND KIND

Flat-Coated Retrievers are known to be sensitive dogs who learn best with gentle but consistent teaching methods. They thrive on praise and knowing that they have pleased their masters. Harsh training methods and physical abuse will not get you the results you want with your Flat-Coat; such treatment will only teach the dog to be afraid of you. Any corrections given to a Flat-Coat must be fair and never harsh.

The Flat-Coat is perhaps best known for its elegant head and sleek black body. Often mistaken for a "slender black Labrador" or a "black Irish Setter," the Flat-Coat nevertheless is a most distinguished-looking dog with classic features. He is a graceful but strong dog with a distinctive long head, an intelligent expression and a dense, well-feathered coat. Known for his long, racy body and smooth, ground-covering action, he combines ineffable beauty with unspoiled utility. He is extremely versatile, being a hunting retriever as well as a responsive and congenial family companion who is able to achieve high levels of proficiency in a variety of endeavors.

EXERCISE AND COMPANIONSHIP

An active dog that adapts well to country, suburban or city life, the Flat-Coat requires considerable daily activity and exercise with family members no matter where he lives. This is a clean, energetic and cheerful dog who keeps his youthful outlook on life well into old age. Although he's a typical retriever who is gentle and affectionate and always ready to play, he has a higher activity level than a Golden or Labrador Retriever. A properly bred Flat-Coat will be highly energetic, but not hyper. His need for exercise is enormous and, without it, he will become destructive and difficult to control. Even with adequate exercise, he will remain exuberant and enthusiastic, always ready to leap into some new activity with you. "Sedate" is not part of his job description!

The Flat-Coat definitely needs to be with people and requires close interaction with members of his family. He will become frustrated if separated from his "pack" and will not thrive if confined to a doghouse in his owner's back yard. Because of their high energy level, Flat-Coats become bored easily and can become "creatively destructive" if left unsupervised too long without something to occupy their time. Like other retrievers, they are very oral dogs who seem obsessed with always having something in their mouths to carry around.

Being retrievers, Flat-Coats can easily be trained and exercised simultaneously. Pet shops sell retrieving dummies to help train your Flat-Coat; the dog will enjoy the activity.

LEFT: A luxurious, healthy, shiny coat is the result of good health and attention to grooming. RIGHT: The Labrador Retriever, shown here, has a shorter coat and a bulkier body, but it is easy to see why the two breeds are often confused.

What a catch! The athletic and agile Flat-Coat has lots of energy to expend, and what better way to do so than by playing retrieving games with his favorite person?

Flat-Coats as a breed make poor watchdogs. Perhaps more of a warning dog than a watchdog, he will bark at a stranger but rarely bite. He is basically a tail-wagging fellow who is inclined to be friendly to everyone, animals as well as people. Although he is good with children, he can be a hazard around small children because of his exuberance and strength. His joyful attitude and wildly wagging tail can unintentionally intimidate or even harm young children, who could be easily injured by 60 or so pounds of canine enthusiasm. A common Flat-Coat greeting is jumping up for a happy hello and nose-to-nose lick in the face, a typical behavior that few adults appreciate or condone.

DON'T WANNA GROW UP!

You should allow plenty of time for your Flat-Coat to grow up. Flat-Coats are very slow to mature and will remain puppy-like well into their third and fourth years.

COAT MANAGEMENT

Although the Flat-Coat carries a double coat and sheds his hair indiscriminately, his coat is smoother and less feathered than the heavy-coated Golden Retriever and thus requires much less grooming. Frequent (with an emphasis on "frequent") brushing will keep his coat in good condition and keep the shedding to a minimum.

MATURITY AND TRAINING

Most notably, the Flat-Coat is very slow to mature physically and emotionally, and doesn't outgrow his puppy nature until he's three or four years of age. Early puppy training is essential and encouraged, although training must be kept brief and happy, because the breed's sensitive nature will resist heavy-handed tactics. Flat-Coats are bright and eager students who learn quickly and easily, but can also become shy and fearful if they are harshly treated. In training they require a light but firm technique and, above all, an individual approach. Proper behavior should be encouraged and good manners strictly enforced through short, positive, upbeat lessons. Bad habits can be prevented with proper supervision, attention and adequate exercise.

While the Flat-Coat is enthusiastic about working, he also can be equally stubborn, especially if he is treated harshly or unfairly (in his opinion). He requires a good foundation in obedience offered at a very early age in order to become a civilized dog and a well-behaved companion.

The Flat-Coat loves his people and he's not afraid to show it.

Even when young, the Flat-Coat will show a love of water.

Although a Flat-Coat must be introduced to training early in life to prevent unruliness and for the owner to gain control, training can also present unusual challenges. Because this is a slow-maturing dog who is still a puppy at 12, even 24 months of age, he is not capable of the same high degree of proficiency one would expect in a Border Collie or a Golden Retriever of the same age. Never train for too long or with a stern attitude. Training this breed can easily test the patience and determination of an owner who cannot accept a full-grown dog who continues to act like he's still a silly pup. But if you are cheerful and enthusiastic, your Flat-Coat will be, too.

TASKS AND ABILITIES

The Flat-Coated Retriever is versatile and can be trained for a multitude of sports and jobs. Many Flat-Coats enjoy success in agility and obedience competition. Of course, the breed's traditional pursuit is to assist hunters by retrieving on land or in water. Dogs not used in this capacity can develop their instinctive skills through training for field trials and/or hunting events. The Flat-Coat is a talented swimmer and will enjoy the opportunity to get some of his activity in the water if possible. The Flat-Coat's abilities have proved useful in various types of service as well.

Flat-Coats, because they are slow to mature emotionally, have to be trained in a gentle manner or they will become shy and fearful. Once matured and trained, they are wonderful pets and companions.

Guide and Assistance Dogs

As a general rule, Flat-Coats are considered too active for work as guide dogs for the blind, hearing dogs for the deaf or service animals for the physically challenged. The most successful results have been with Flat-Coats who have been trained to help their partially sighted owners, people who already know and love their dog.

Tracking

Flat-Coats, like the other retriever breeds, are known for superior scenting ability. As "super sniffers," they have nosed their way into most of today's tracking and scenting adventures. In some countries, the Flat-Coated Retriever participates in regulated tracking events, earning tracking titles in

The multi-talented and friendly Flat-Coat easily becomes a true member of his owner's family.

formal competition.

Flat-Coats accomplished in tracking venues are also used in some countries to track wounded animals such as deer and elk who have been injured in road or hunting accidents. In Norway, for example, it is forbidden by law to hunt deer or elk without the presence of an officially registered tracking dog.

Search and Rescue

In several countries Flat-Coats also follow their noses to find lost, injured and buried people. Flat-Coats have been trained for avalanche work and are adept at locating humans buried under huge mounds of snow. Such dogs work under extreme conditions; their ability to work in heavy snow and freezing weather underscores their scenting prowess.

Search and rescue Flat-Coats also assist in locating victims of natural disasters such as earthquakes and of terrorist disasters such as bomb explosion sites.

Drug Detection

Not surprisingly, Flat-Coats have also proven to be outstanding sniffer dogs for drugs. At one time during the 1990s in Norway, Flat-Coated Retrievers totaled one-third of that country's approved canine drug-detection force. Although the breed in Norway is considered to be hyperactive, that very characteristic is felt to contribute to the breed's superior working capability.

BREED STANDARD FOR THE

FLAT-COATED RETRIEVER

A standard is a written description of what the ideal representative of a breed should look, act and move like. The perfect dog described in a breed standard does not exist, even though some breed standards were "based upon" an existing champion that was popular or considered ideal at that time. Composing such a word picture is fraught with difficulty and dissension, since words are prone to interpretation and the meanings of words vary. For instance, what is in balance to one viewer is totally out of balance to the next. Thus breeders and judges could never agree on the perfect dog even if it walked into the show ring! Nonetheless, the breed standard is the best measuring stick available for determining which Flat-Coats are excellent and which are below average. The standard is used by judges in the show ring, just as breeders use the standard to decide which dogs are worth breeding and which dogs are not.

For the pet owner who has no intention of showing or breeding his dog, the question pops into mind: should I skip this chapter and get on with the puppy chapter? The author answers with a qualified *no!* Even though you are not terribly concerned about the "standard of perfection" for your trustworthy chum, you are interested in your Flat-Coat's temperament and personality, which are described in detail in the standard along with physical traits. If you were not interested in the Flat-Coat as a breed and what makes the breed what it is, you probably would not be reading this book. There is no sense in selecting a Flat-Coated Retriever that doesn't look and behave like a Flat-Coat. Pet owners are encouraged to use the breed standard to confirm what a Flat-Coat really should be! The physical and temperamental attributes that attract the pet owner to the Flat-Coat are precisely defined in the breed standard. It is provided here for the reference of everyone interested in the Flat-Coat breed.

THE AMERICAN KENNEL CLUB STANDARD FOR THE FLAT-COATED RETRIEVER

General Appearance: The Flat-Coated Retriever is a versatile family companion hunting retriever with a happy and active demeanor, intelligent expression, and clean lines. The Flat-Coat has been traditionally described as showing *"power without lumber and raciness without weediness."*

The distinctive and most important features of the Flat-Coat are the silhouette (both moving and standing), smooth effortless movement, head type, coat and character. In silhouette the Flat-Coat has a long, strong, clean, "one piece" head, which is unique to the breed. Free from exaggeration of stop or cheek, the head is set well into a moderately long neck which flows smoothly into well laid back shoulders. A level topline combined with a deep, long rib cage tapering to a moderate tuck-up create the impression of a blunted triangle. The brisket is well developed and the forechest forms a prominent prow. This utilitarian retriever is well balanced, strong, but elegant; never cobby, short legged or rangy. The coat is thick and flat lying, and the legs and tail are well feathered. A proud carriage, responsive attitude, waving tail and overall look of functional strength, quality, style and symmetry complete the picture of the typical Flat-Coat.

Judging the Flat-Coat moving freely on a loose lead and standing naturally is more important than judging him posed. Honorable scars should not count against the dog.

Size, Proportion, Substance: ***Size—*** Individuals varying more than an inch either way from the preferred height should be considered not practical for the types of work for which the Flat-Coat was developed. Preferred height is 23 to 24.5; inches at the withers for dogs, 22 to 23.5 inches for bitches. Since the Flat-Coat is a working hunting retriever he should be shown in lean, hard condition, free of excess weight.

Proportion—The Flat-Coat is not cobby in build. The length of the body from the point of the shoulder to the rearmost projection of the upper thigh is slightly more than the height at the withers. The female may be slightly longer to better accommodate the carrying of puppies. ***Substance—*** Moderate. Medium bone is flat or oval rather than round; strong but never massive, coarse, weedy or fine. This applies throughout the dog.

Head: The long, clean, well molded head is adequate in size and strength to retrieve a large pheasant, duck or hare with ease. ***Skull and Muzzle—***The impression of the

The breed standard is the written description of the ideal dog. There is no perfect dog that exactly matches the standard; rather, the standard provides a blueprint for breeders and judges.

skull and muzzle being "cast in one piece" is created by the fairly flat skull of moderate breadth and flat, clean cheeks, combined with the long, strong, deep muzzle which is well filled in before, between and beneath the eyes. Viewed from above, the muzzle is nearly equal in length and breadth to the skull. *Stop*—There is a gradual, slight, barely perceptible stop, avoiding a down or dish-faced appearance. Brows are slightly raised and mobile, giving life to the expression. Stop must be evaluated in profile so that it will not be confused with the raised brow. *Occiput* not accentuated, the skull forming a gentle curve where it fits well into the neck. ***Expression*** alert, intelligent and kind. ***Eyes*** are set widely apart. Medium sized, almond shaped, dark brown or hazel; not large, round or yellow. Eye rims are self-colored and tight. ***Ears*** relatively small, well set on, lying close to the side of the head and thickly feathered. Not low set (houndlike or setterish). ***Nose***—Large open nostrils. Black on black dogs, brown on liver dogs. ***Lips*** fairly tight, firm, clean and dry to minimize the retention of feathers. ***Jaws*** long and strong, capable of carrying a hare or a pheasant. ***Bite***—Scissors bite preferred, level bite acceptable. Broken teeth should not count against the dog. ***Severe Faults***—Wry and undershot or overshot bites with a noticeable gap must be severely penalized.

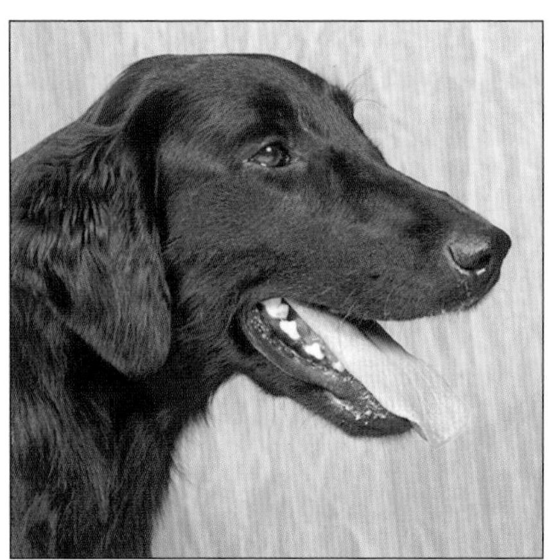

The nicely shaped head, strong and long, is suitable for carrying small game. The ears are small and close-lying.

Neck, Topline, Body: ***Neck*** strong and slightly arched for retrieving strength. Moderately long to allow for easy seeking of the trail. Free from throatiness. Coat on neck is untrimmed. ***Topline*** strong and level. ***Body***—*Chest (Brisket)*—Deep, reaching to the elbow and only moderately broad. *Forechest*—Prow prominent and well developed. *Rib cage* deep, showing good length from forechest to last rib (to allow ample space for all body organs), and only moderately broad. The foreribs fairly flat showing a gradual spring, well arched in the center of the body but rather lighter towards the loin. *Underline*—Deep chest tapering to a moderate *tuck-up. Loin* strong, well muscled and long enough to allow for agility, freedom of movement and length of stride, but never weak or loosely coupled. *Croup* slopes very slightly; rump moderately broad and well muscled. ***Tail*** fairly straight, well set on, with bone reaching approximately to the hock joint. When the dog is in motion, the tail is carried happily but without curl as a smooth extension of the topline, never much above the level of the back.

Forequarters: *Shoulders* long, well laid back shoulder blade with *upper arm* of approximately equal length to allow for efficient reach. Musculature wiry rather than bulky. *Elbows* clean, close to the body and set well back under the withers. *Forelegs* straight and strong with medium bone of good quality. *Pasterns* slightly sloping and strong. *Dewclaws*—Removal of dewclaws is optional. *Feet* oval or round. Medium sized and tight with well arched toes and thick pads.

Hindquarters: Powerful with angulation in balance with the front assembly. *Upper thighs* powerful and well muscled. *Stifle*—Good turn of stifle with sound, strong joint. *Second thighs* (Stifle to hock joint)—Second or lower thigh as long as or only slightly longer than upper thight. *Hock*—Hock joint strong, well let down. *Dewclaws*—There are no hind dewclaws. *Feet* oval or round. Medium sized and tight with well arched toes and thick pads.

Coat: Coat is of moderate length, density and fullness, with a high luster. The ideal coat is straight and flat lying. A slight waviness is permissible but the coat is not curly, wooly, short, silky or fluffy. The Flat-Coat is a working retriever and the coat must provide protection from all types of weather, water and ground cover. This requires a coat of sufficient texture, length and fullness to allow for adequate insulation. When the dog is in full coat the ears, front, chest, back of forelegs, thighs and underside of tail are thickly feathered without being bushy, stringy or silky. Mane of longer heavier coat on the neck extending over the withers and shoulders is considered typical, especially in the male dog, and can

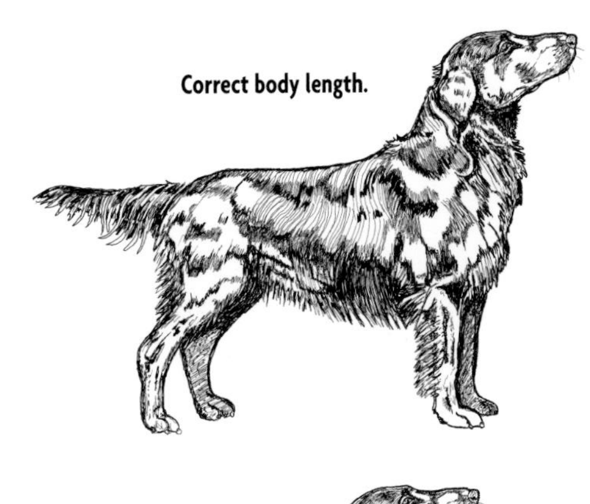

Correct body length.

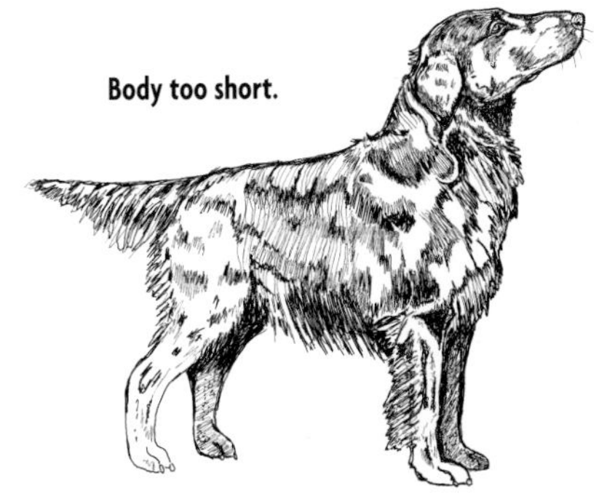

Body too short.

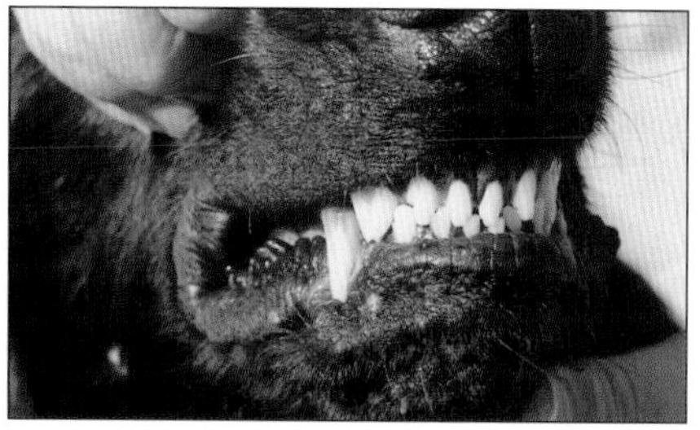

A scissor bite, shown here, is the preferred bite, although a level bite is acceptable.

cause the neck to appear thicker and the withers higher, sometimes causing the appearance of a dip behind the withers. Since the Flat-Coat is a hunting retriever, the feathering is not excessively long. ***Trimming***—The Flat-Coat is shown with as natural a coat as possible and must not be penalized for lack of trimming, as long as the coat is clean and well brushed. Tidying of ears, feet, underline and tip of tail is acceptable. Whiskers serve a specific function and it is preferred that they not be trimmed. Shaving or barbering of the head, neck or body coat must be severely penalized.

Color: Solid black or solid liver. ***Disqualification***—Yellow, cream or any color other than black or liver.

Gait: Sound, efficient movement is of critical importance to a hunting retriever. The Flat-Coat viewed from the side covers ground efficiently and movement appears balanced, free flowing and well coordinated, never choppy, mincing or ponderous. Front and rear legs reach well forward and extend well back, achieving long clean strides. Topline appears level, strong and supple while dog is in motion.

Summary: The Flat-Coat is a strong but elegant, cheerful hunting retriever. Quality of structure, balance and harmony of all parts both standing and in motion are essential. As a breed whose purpose is of a utilitarian nature, structure, condition and attitude should give every indication of being suited for hard work.

Temperament: Character is a primary and outstanding asset of the Flat-Coat. He is a responsive, loving member of the family, a versatile working dog, multi-talented, sensible, bright and tractable. In competition the Flat-Coat demonstrates *stability* and a desire to please with a confident, happy and outgoing attitude characterized by a wagging tail. Nervous, hyperactive, apathetic, shy or obstinate behavior is undesirable. ***Severe Fault***—Unprovoked aggressive behavior toward people or animals is *totally* unacceptable.

Character: Character is as important to the evaluation of stock by a potential breeder as any other aspect of the breed standard. The Flat-Coat is primarily a family companion hunting retriever. He is keen and birdy, flushing within gun range, as well as a determined, resourceful retriever on land and water. He has a great desire to hunt with self-reliance and an uncanny ability to adapt to changing circumstances on a variety of upland game and waterfowl.

As a family companion he is sensible, alert and highly intelligent; a lighthearted, affectionate and adaptable friend. He retains these qualities as well as his youthfully good-humored outlook on life into old age. The adult Flat-Coat is usually an adequate alarm dog to give warning, but is a good-natured, optimistic dog, basically inclined to be friendly to all.

The Flat-Coat is a cheerful, devoted companion who requires and appreciates living with and interacting as a member of his family. To reach full potential in any endeavor he absolutely must have a strong personal bond and affectionate individual attention.

Disqualification: *Yellow, cream or any color other than black or liver.*

Approved September 11, 1990
Effective October 30, 1990

NOTES ON THE STANDARD

In order to appreciate a breed standard, you must understand the purpose for which it was created in the first place. Breed standards are intended to preserve and promote the integrity of a breed and its purpose in the canine-human scheme.

The emphasis on structural qualities is intended to preserve the original purpose of the Flat-Coat: to hunt well, locate game, retrieve it and gently deliver it to hand. Its elegant head type is no accident: the properly proportioned head with a correct bite, muzzle, lips and flews is of prime importance in the business of retrieving ducks, pheasant or hare. Even eye placement and ear set have a distinct purpose in a dog who spends his time afield. A body designed for speed and power enhances the Flat-Coat's performance in the field. The sleek, dense coat that insulates the Flat-Coat working gundog from wind or icy water also creates the elegance so admired in the show ring.

Liver is one of the two acceptable colors in the Flat-Coated Retriever.

FLAT-COATED RETRIEVER

OWNER QUALIFICATIONS

Not every dog lover is properly equipped to live with a Flat-Coated Retriever or provide him with the type of home or environment he requires to live a quality life. The quality of the owner's life also becomes questionable, since an unhappy Flat-Coat will surely become disruptive and out of control.

If you are contemplating a future with Flat-Coats, you should look deep into your dog-loving soul and ask yourself if you are willing to do the following:

- Live with the hair, constant retrieving and other high-energy activities for the dog's entire lifetime, which should be a decade or more.
- Have the patience and endurance to accept and, yes, enjoy the trials and tribulations of living with a grown-up puppy for four or five years.
- Accept the responsibility for all future life changes, the dog's and your own, including such events as new babies, children in school or moving to a new home.
- Give your Flat-Coat several hours of attention and exercise each and every day.
- Train your Flat-Coat to become a well-behaved family member who would be welcome anywhere in your community.
- Provide proper veterinary care, including annual check-ups, vaccinations, spaying or neutering and emergency health care. Can you afford it and are you willing to spend the money?
- Keep your Flat-Coat safe at all times, whether in the house, yard or car. This includes never chaining him outside or permiting him to ride loose in an open truck.
- Become educated about the proper care of the Flat-Coat breed, correct training methods and good grooming habits.
- Consult your breeder or other dog professional if you have questions or problems before things spin out of control.
- Accept full responsibility for the dog's well-being regardless of his age, infirmity, future disability or health problems.
- Take whatever time necessary to find a responsible breeder and select the right puppy for your family.

If you've answered "Yes" to all of these questions, you are

ready to begin life as a Flat-Coated Retriever owner. Start your puppy search early, as most good breeders often have waiting lists. Don't rush into the purchase of a pup and don't become discouraged by a wait. The right puppy is always worth waiting for!

WHERE TO BEGIN?

If you are convinced that the Flat-Coat is the ideal dog for you, it's time to learn about where to find a puppy and what to look for. Locating a litter of Flat-Coats will require more research than finding Labradors or Golden Retrievers. You should inquire about breeders in your area who enjoy a good reputation in the breed. You are looking for an established breeder with outstanding dog ethics and a strong commitment to the breed. New owners should have as many questions as they have doubts. An established breeder is indeed the one to answer your four million questions and make you comfortable with your choice of the Flat-Coat. An established breeder will sell you a puppy at a fair price if, and only if, the breeder determines that you are a suitable worthy owner of his/her dogs. An established breeder can be relied upon for advice, at any reasonable time. A reputable breeder will accept a puppy back, often without any penalty to you, should you decide that this is not the right dog for you.

FINDING A QUALIFIED BREEDER

Before you begin your puppy search, ask for references from your veterinarian and perhaps other breeders to refer you to someone they believe is reputable. Responsible breeders usually raise only one or two breeds of dog. Avoid any breeder who has several different breeds or has several litters at the same time. Dedicated breeders are usually involved with a breed or other dog club. Many participate in some sport or activity related to their breed. Just as you want to be assured of the breeder's qualifications, the breeder wants to be assured that you will make a worthy owner. Expect the breeder to interview you, asking questions about your goals for the pup, your experience with dogs and what kind of home you will provide.

When choosing a breeder, reputation is much more important than convenience of location. Do not be overly impressed by breeders who run brag advertisements in the canine publications about their stupendous champions and working lines. The real quality breeders are quiet and unassuming. You hear about them at trials and shows, by word of mouth. You may be well advised to avoid the novice who lives only a few miles away. The local novice breeder, trying so hard to get rid of that first litter of puppies, is more than accommodating and anxious to sell you one. That breeder will charge you as much as any established breeder. The novice breeder isn't going to interrogate you and your family about your intentions with the puppy, the environment and training you can provide, etc. That breeder will be nowhere to be found when your poorly bred, badly adjusted four-pawed monster starts to growl and spit up at midnight or eat the family cat!

SIGNS OF A HEALTHY PUPPY

Healthy puppies are robust little fellows who are alert and active, sporting shiny coats and supple skin. They should not appear lethargic, bloated or pot-bellied, nor should they have flaky skin or runny or crusted eyes or noses. Their stools should be firm and well formed, with no evidence of blood or mucus.

A Flat-Coat puppy is a bundle of puppy exuberance and affection, sure to bring fun and joy to owners who can give him the care he needs.

Choosing a breeder is an important first step in dog ownership. Fortunately, the majority of Flat-Coat breeders are devoted to the breed and its well-being. New owners should have little problem finding a reputable breeder who doesn't live on the other side of the country. The American Kennel Club and Flat-Coated Retriever Society of America are trusted sources of breeder referrals. Potential owners are encouraged to attend shows and events like obedience and hunting tests to see the Flat-Coats in action, to meet the owners and handlers firsthand and to get an idea of what Flat-Coats look like outside a photographer's lens. Provided you approach the owners and they are not busy with the dogs, most are more than willing to answer questions, recommend breeders and give advice.

Once you have contacted and met a breeder or two and made your choice about which breeder is best suited to your needs, it's time to visit the litter. Again, keep in mind that many top breeders have waiting lists. Sometimes new owners have to wait over a year for a puppy. If you are really committed to the breeder whom you've selected, then you will wait (and hope for an early arrival!). If not, you may have to go with your second- or third-choice breeder. Don't be too anxious, however.

Since you are likely to be choosing a Flat-Coat as a pet dog and not a hunting or show dog, you simply should select a pup that is healthy, sound, friendly and attractive. While the basic structure and temperament of the breed has little variation, personality will vary among individual pups. Beware of the shy or overly aggressive puppy; be especially conscious of the nervous Flat-Coat pup. Don't let sentiment or

SELECTING FROM THE LITTER

Before you visit a litter of puppies, promise yourself that you won't fall for the first pretty face you see! Decide on your goals for your puppy—show prospect, hunting dog, obedience competitor, family companion—and then look for a puppy who displays the appropriate qualities. In most litters, there is an Alpha pup (the bossy puppy), and occasionally a shy fellow who is less confident, with the rest of the litter falling somewhere in the middle. "Middle-of-the-roaders" are safe bets for most families and novice competitors.

GETTING ACQUAINTED

When visiting a litter, ask the breeder for suggestions on how best to interact with the puppies. If possible, get right into the middle of the pack and sit down with them. Observe which pups climb into your lap and which ones shy away. Toss a toy for them to chase and bring back to you. It's easy to fall in love with the puppy who picks you, but keep your future objectives in mind before you make your final decision.

emotion trap you into buying the runt of the litter.

If you have intentions of your new pup hunting ground birds or hare, there are other considerations. The parents of a future hunting dog should have excellent qualifications, including actual field experience as well as field titles in their pedigrees. For any kind of pup, pet, show or hunting, titles in the pedigree are signs of good breeding.

Breeders commonly allow visitors to see the litter by around the fifth or sixth week, and puppies leave for their new homes between the eighth and tenth week. Breeders who permit their puppies to leave early are more interested in a profit than in their puppies' well-being. Puppies need to learn the rules of the trade from their dams, and most dams continue teaching the pups manners and "dos and don'ts" until at least the eighth week. Breeders spend significant amounts of time with the Flat-Coat pups so that they are able to interact with the "other species," i.e., humans. Given the long history that dogs and humans have, bonding between the two species is natural but must be nurtured. A well-bred, well-socialized Flat-Coat pup wants nothing more than to be near you and to please you.

A COMMITTED NEW OWNER

By now you should understand what makes the Flat-Coated Retriever a most unique and special dog, one that may fit nicely into your family and lifestyle. If you have researched breeders, you should be able to recognize a knowledgeable and responsible Flat-Coated Retriever breeder who cares not only about his pups but also about what kind of owner you will be. If you have completed the final step in your new journey, you have found a litter, or possibly two, of quality Flat-Coated Retriever pups.

A visit with the puppies and their breeder should be an education in itself. Breed research, breeder selection and puppy visitation are very important aspects of finding the puppy of your dreams. Beyond that, these things also lay the foundation for a successful future with your pup. Puppy personalities within each litter vary, from the shy and easygoing puppy to the one who is dominant and assertive, with most pups falling somewhere in between. By spending time with the puppies, you will be able to recognize certain behaviors and what these behaviors indicate about each pup's temperament. Which type of pup will complement your family dynamics is best determined by observing the puppies in action within their "pack." Your breeder's expertise and recommendations are also valuable. Although you may fall in love with a bold and brassy male, the breeder may suggest that another pup would be best for you. The breeder's experience in rearing Flat-Coated Retriever pups and

A happy Flat-Coat puppy is a Flat-Coat puppy with a toy in his mouth!

PEDIGREE VS. REGISTRATION CERTIFICATE

Too often new owners are confused between these two important documents. Your puppy's pedigree, essentially a family tree, is a written record of a dog's genealogy of three generations or more. The pedigree will show you the names as well as performance titles of all dogs in your pup's background. Your breeder must provide you with a registration application, with his part properly filled out. You must complete the application and send it to the AKC with the proper fee. Every puppy must come from a litter that has been AKC-registered by the breeder, born in the US and from a sire and dam that are also registered with the AKC.

The seller must provide you with complete records to identify the puppy. The AKC requires that the seller provide the buyer with the following: breed; sex, color and markings; date of birth; litter number (when available); names and registration numbers of the parents; breeder's name; and date sold or delivered.

THE FAMILY TREE

Your puppy's pedigree is his family tree. Just as a child may resemble his parents and grandparents, so too will a puppy reflect the qualities, good and bad, of his ancestors, especially those in the first two generations. Therefore it's important to know as much as possible about a puppy's immediate relatives. Reputable and experienced breeders should be able to explain the pedigree and why they chose to breed from the particular dogs they used.

The pup you choose should look healthy and alert, with a shiny coat and clear eyes.

matching their temperaments with appropriate humans offers the best assurance that your pup will meet your needs and expectations. The type of puppy that you select is just as important as your decision that the Flat-Coat is the breed for you.

The decision to live with a Flat-Coated Retriever is a serious commitment and not one to be taken lightly. This puppy is a living sentient being that will be dependent on you for basic survival for his entire life. Beyond the basics of survival—food, water, shelter and protection—he needs much, much more. The new pup needs love, nurturing and a proper canine education to mold him into a responsible, well-behaved canine citizen. Your Flat-Coat's health and good manners will need consistent monitoring and regular "tune-ups," so your job as a responsible dog owner will be ongoing throughout every stage of his life. If you are not prepared to accept these responsibilities and commit to them for the next decade, likely longer, then you are not prepared to own a dog of any breed.

Although the responsibilities of owning a dog may at times tax your patience, the joy of living with your Flat-Coat far outweighs the workload, and a well-mannered adult dog is worth your time and effort. Before your very eyes, your new charge will grow up to be your most loyal friend, devoted to you unconditionally.

YOUR FLAT-COATED RETRIEVER SHOPPING LIST

Just as expectant parents prepare a nursery for their baby, so should you ready your home for the arrival of your Flat-Coated Retriever pup. If you have the necessary puppy supplies purchased and in place before he comes home, it will ease the puppy's transition from the warmth and familiarity of his mom and littermates to the brand-new environment of his new home and human family. You will be too busy to stock up and prepare your house after your pup comes home, that's for sure! Imagine how a pup must feel upon being transported to a strange new place. It's up to you to comfort him and to let your little pup know that he is going to be happy with you.

PUPPY PARASITES

Parasites are nasty little critters that live in or on your dog or puppy. Most puppies are born with ascarid roundworms, which are acquired from dormant ascarids residing in the dam. Other parasites can be acquired through contact with infected fecal matter. Take a stool sample to your vet for testing. He will prescribe a safe wormer to treat any parasites found in your puppy's stool. Always have a fecal test performed at your puppy's annual veterinary exam.

The bowls you choose for your Flat-Coat should be sturdy, chew-proof and easy to clean.

Food and Water Bowls

Your puppy will need separate bowls for his food and water. Stainless steel pans are generally preferred over plastic bowls since they sterilize better and pups are less inclined to chew on the metal. Heavy-duty ceramic bowls are popular, but consider how often you will have to pick up those heavy bowls. Buy adult-sized pans, as your Flat-Coat puppy will grow into them before you know it.

The Dog Crate

If you think that crates are tools of punishment and confinement for when a dog has misbehaved, think again. Most breeders and almost all trainers recommend a crate as the preferred house-training aid as well as for all-around puppy training and safety.

COST OF OWNERSHIP
The purchase price of your puppy is merely the first expense in the typical dog budget. Quality dog food, veterinary care (sickness and health maintenance), dog supplies and grooming costs will add up to big bucks every year. Can you adequately afford to support a canine addition to the family?

Because dogs are natural den creatures that prefer cave-like environments, the benefits of crate use are many. The crate provides the puppy with his very own "safe house," a cozy place to sleep, take a break or seek comfort with a favorite toy; a travel aid to house your dog when on the road, at motels or at the vet's office; a training aid to help teach your puppy proper toileting habits; a place of solitude when non-dog people happen to drop by and don't want a lively puppy—or even a well-behaved adult dog—saying hello or begging for attention.

A good breeder invests the same time, care and love into each and every pup, and truly cares about their welfare in their future homes.

Crates come in several types, although the wire crate and the fiberglass airline-type crate are the most popular. Both are safe and your puppy will adjust to either one, so the choice is up to you. The wire crates offer better visibility for the pup as well as better ventilation. Many of the wire crates fold down to make them easy to carry. The fiberglass crates, similar to those used by the airlines for animal transport, are sturdier and more den-like. However, the fiberglass crates do not collapse and are less ventilated than a wire crate, which can be problematic in hot weather. Some of the newer crates are made of heavy plastic mesh; they are very lightweight and fold up into slim-line suitcases. However, a mesh crate might not be suitable for a pup with manic chewing habits.

Don't bother with a puppy-sized crate. Although your Flat-Coated Retriever will be a wee fellow when you bring him home, he will grow up in the blink of an eye and your puppy crate will be useless. Purchase a crate that will accommodate an adult Flat-

Coated Retriever. With his adult size in mind, a large crate, measuring about 42 inches long by 28 inches wide by 32 inches high, will fit him nicely. Removable divider panels are available to partition off a smaller section for the pup to facilitate house-training.

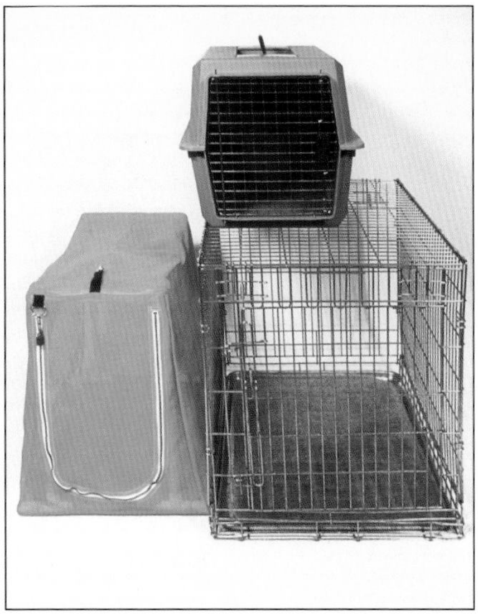

Your local pet-supply shop usually carries a variety of crates from which you can select one that best suits your needs.

Bedding and Crate Pads

Your puppy will enjoy some type of soft bedding in his "room" (the crate), something he can snuggle into to feel cozy and secure. Old towels or blankets are good choices for a young pup, since he may (and probably will) have a toileting accident or two in the crate or decide to chew on the bedding material. Once he is fully trained and out of the early chewing stage, you can replace the puppy bedding with a permanent crate pad if you prefer. Crate pads and other dog beds run the gamut from inexpensive to high-end doggie-designer styles, but don't splurge on the good stuff until you are sure that your puppy is reliable and won't tear it up or make a mess on it.

Crate Expectations

To make the crate more inviting to your puppy, you can offer his first meal or two inside the crate, always keeping the crate door open so that he does not feel confined. Keep a favorite toy or two in the crate for him to play with while inside. You can also cover the crate at night with a lightweight sheet to make it more den-like and remove the stimuli of household activity. Never put him into his crate as punishment or as you are scolding him, since he will then associate his crate with negative situations and avoid going there.

Puppy Toys

Just as infants and older children require objects to stimulate their minds and bodies, puppies need toys to entertain their curious brains, wiggly paws and achy teeth. A fun array of safe doggie toys will help satisfy your puppy's chewing instincts and distract him from gnawing on the leg of your antique chair or your new leather sofa. Most puppy toys are cute and look as if they would be a lot of fun, but not all are necessarily safe or good for your puppy, so use caution when you go puppy-toy shopping.

Flat-Coat puppies, being retrievers, are orally obsessed and seem to be always putting something in their mouths. The best "chewcifiers" are nylon and hard rubber bones which are safe to gnaw on and come in sizes appropriate for all age groups and breeds. Be especially careful of natural bones, which can splinter or develop dangerous sharp edges; pups can easily swallow or choke on those bone splinters. Veterinarians often tell of surgical nightmares involving bits of splintered bone, because in addition to the danger of choking, the sharp pieces can damage the intestinal tract.

Similarly, rawhide chews, while a favorite of most dogs and puppies, can be equally dangerous. Pieces of rawhide are easily swallowed after they get soft and gummy from chewing,

One of the first things your puppy should learn is that the crate is his refuge.

and dogs have been known to choke on large pieces of ingested rawhide. Rawhide chews should be offered only when you can supervise the puppy.

Soft woolly toys are special puppy favorites. They come in a wide variety of cute shapes and sizes; some look like little stuffed animals. Flat-Coat puppies (and sometimes adults) often love to carry around their favorite stuffed toys. Be careful of fuzzy toys that have button eyes or noses that your pup could chew off and swallow, and make sure that he does not disembowel a squeaky toy to remove the squeaker! Braided rope toys are similar in that they are fun to chew and toss around, but they shred easily and the strings are easy to swallow. The strings are not digestible and, if the puppy doesn't pass them in his stool, he could end up at the vet's office. As with rawhides, your puppy should be closely monitored with rope toys.

If you believe that your pup has ingested a piece of one of his toys, check his stools for the next couple of days to see if he passes the item when he defecates. At the same time, also watch for signs of intestinal distress. A call to your veterinarian might be in order to get his advice and be on the safe side.

An all-time favorite toy for puppies (young and old!) is the empty gallon milk jug. Hard

TOYS 'R SAFE

The vast array of tantalizing puppy toys is staggering. Stroll through any pet shop or pet-supply outlet and you will see that the choices can be overwhelming. However, not all dog toys are safe or sensible. Most Flat-Coat puppies enjoy soft woolly toys that they can snuggle with and carry around. (You know they have outgrown them when they shred them up!) Avoid toys that have buttons, tabs or other enhancements that can be chewed off and swallowed. Soft toys that squeak are fun, but make sure your puppy does not disembowel the toy and remove (and swallow) the squeaker. Toys that rattle or make noise can excite a puppy, but they present the same danger as the squeaky kind and so require supervision. Hard rubber toys that bounce can also entertain a pup, but make sure that the toy is too big for your pup to swallow.

All retriever breeds are mouth-oriented dogs. They love to carry things and, even more, to chew on anything they can find. You must provide your pup with safe chew devices and keep any dangerous or otherwise forbidden items out of his reach.

plastic juice containers—46 ounces or more—are also excellent. Such containers make lots of noise when they are batted about, and puppies go crazy with delight as they play with them. However, they don't often last very long, so be sure to remove and replace them when they get chewed up. The same rule goes for any toys that are excessively chewed, thus potentially dangerous.

A word of caution about homemade toys: be careful with your choices of non-traditional play objects. Never use old shoes or socks, since a puppy cannot distinguish between the old ones on which he's allowed to chew and the new ones in your closet that are strictly off limits. That principle applies to anything that resembles something that you don't want your puppy to chew.

Collars

A lightweight nylon collar is the best choice for a very young pup. Quick-clip collars are easy to put on and remove, and they can be adjusted as the puppy grows. Introduce him to his collar as soon as he comes home to get him accustomed to wearing it. He'll get used to it quickly and won't mind a bit. Make sure that it is snug enough that it won't

Collaring Our Canines

The standard flat collar with a buckle or a snap, in leather, nylon or cotton, is widely regarded as the everyday all-purpose collar. If the collar fits correctly, you should be able to fit two fingers between the collar and the dog's neck.

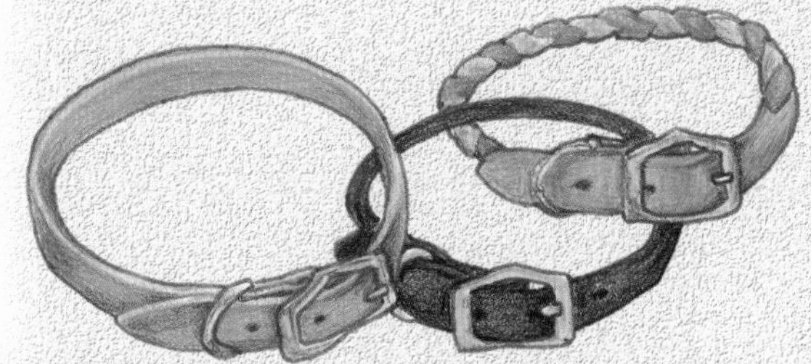

Leather Buckle Collars

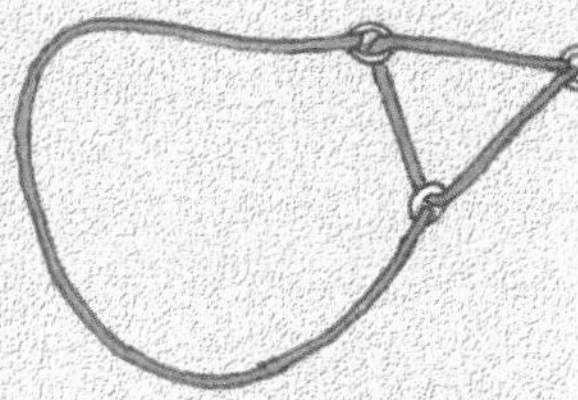

Limited-Slip Collar

The martingale, Greyhound or limited-slip collar is preferred by many dog owners and trainers. It is fixed with an extra loop that tightens when pressure is applied to the leash. The martingale collar gets tighter but does not "choke" the dog. The limited-slip collar should only be used for walking and training, not for free play or interaction with another dog. These types of collar should never be left on the dog, as the extra loop can lead to accidents.

Choke collars, usually made of stainless steel, are made for training purposes but are not recommended for small dogs or heavily coated breeds. The chains can injure small dogs or damage long/abundant coats, and are also considered too harsh for some breeds or individual dogs. Thin nylon choke leads are commonly used on show dogs while in the ring, though they are not practical for everyday use.

Snap Bolt Choke Collar

The harness, with two or three straps that attach over the dog's shoulders and around his torso, is a humane and safe alternative to the conventional collar. By and large, a well-made harness is virtually escape-proof. Harnesses are available in nylon and mesh and can be outfitted on most dogs, with chest girths ranging from 10 to 30 inches.

Harness

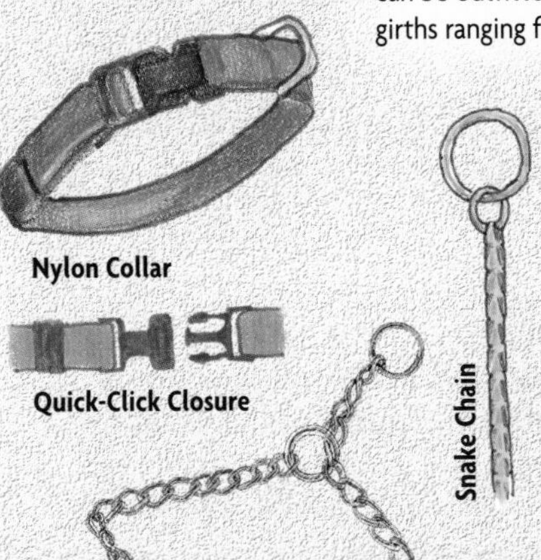

Nylon Collar

Quick-Click Closure

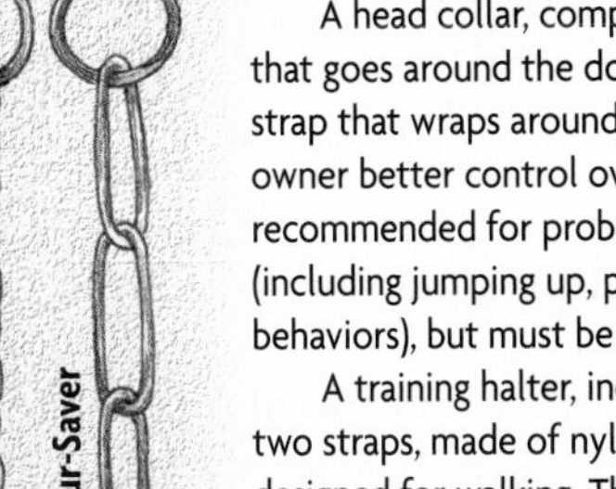

Choke Chain Collars

A head collar, composed of a nylon strap that goes around the dog's muzzle and a second strap that wraps around his neck, offers the owner better control over his dog. This device is recommended for problem-solving with dogs (including jumping up, pulling and aggressive behaviors), but must be used with care.

A training halter, including a flat collar and two straps, made of nylon and webbing, is designed for walking. There are several on the market; some are more difficult to put on the dog than others. The halter harness, with two small slip rings at each end, is recommended for ease of use.

CONFINEMENT

It is wise to keep your puppy confined to a small "puppy-proofed" area of the house for his first few weeks at home. Gate or block off a space near the door he will use for outdoor potty trips. Expandable baby gates are useful to create puppy's designated area. If he is allowed to roam through the entire house or even only several rooms, it will be more difficult to house-train him.

slip off, yet loose enough to be comfortable for the pup. You should be able to slip two fingers between the collar and his neck. Check the collar often, as puppies grow in spurts, and his collar can become too tight almost overnight. Choke collars are for training purposes only, but should never be used on puppies and shouldn't be necessary with a Flat-Coat who has been trained from an early age. The choke collar is often too harsh for the breed, which does better with positive reinforcement rather than correction-based training.

Leashes

A 6-foot nylon lead is an excellent choice for a young puppy. It is lightweight and not as tempting to chew as a leather lead. You can switch to a 6-foot leather lead after your pup has grown and is used to walking politely on a lead. For initial puppy walks and house-training purposes, you should invest in a shorter lead so that you have more control over the puppy. At first, you don't want him wandering too far away from you, and when taking him out for toileting you will want to keep him in the specific area chosen for his potty spot.

Once the puppy is heel-trained with a traditional leash, you can

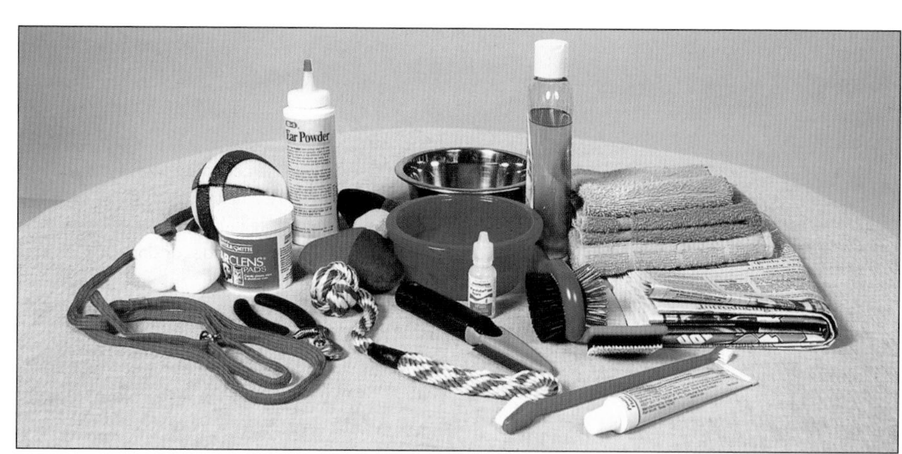

Among the puppy supplies you will need are some good-quality grooming tools, including a brush, nail clippers and canine shampoo.

Leash Life

Dogs love leashes! Believe it or not, most dogs dance for joy every time their owners pick up their leashes. The leash means that the dog is going for a walk—and there are few things more exciting than that! Here are some of the kinds of leashes that are commercially available.

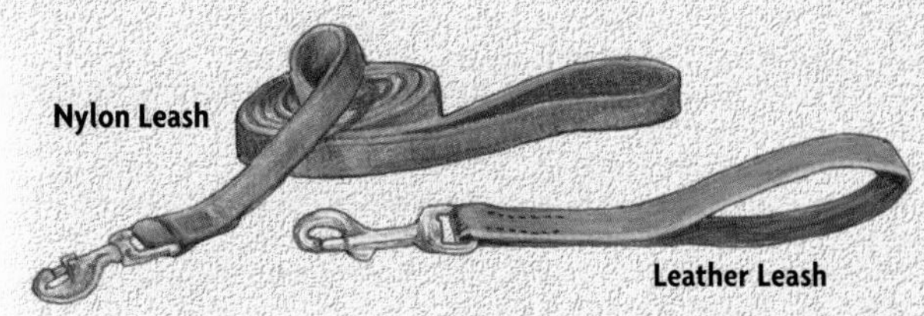

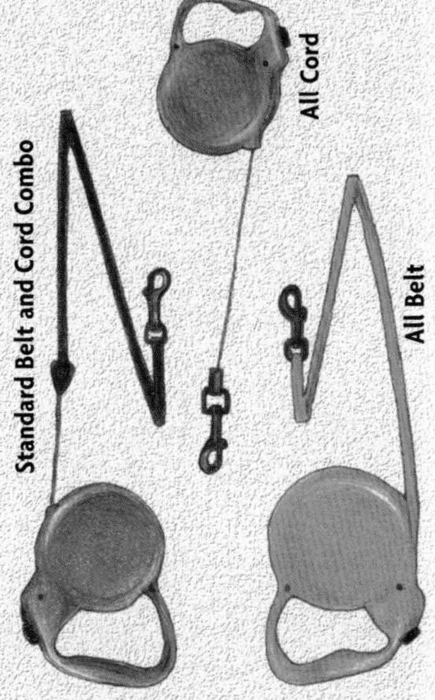

Retractable Leashes

Traditional Leash: Made of cotton, nylon or leather, these leashes are usually about 6 feet in length. A quality-made leather leash is softer on the hands than a nylon one. Durable woven cotton is a popular option. Lengths can vary up to about 48 feet, designed for different uses.

Chain Leash: Usually a metal chain leash with a plastic handle. This is not the best choice for most breeds, as it is heavier than other leashes and difficult to manage.

Retractable Leash: A long nylon cord is housed in a plastic device for extending and retracting. This type of leash is ideal for taking trained dogs for long walks in open areas, although it is not always suitable for large, powerful breeds. Different lengths and sizes are available, so check that you purchase one appropriate for your dog's weight.

Elastic Leash: A nylon leash with an elastic extension. This is useful for well-trained dogs, especially in conjunction with a head halter. Avoid leashes that are completely elastic, as they afford minimal control to the handler.

Adjustable Leash: This has two snaps, one on each end, and several metal rings. It is handy if you need to tether your dog temporarily, but is never to be used with a choke collar.

Tab Leash: A short leash (4 to 6 inches long) that attaches to your dog's collar. This device serves like a handle, in case you have to grab your dog while he's exercising off lead. It's ideal for "half-trained" dogs or dogs that listen only half of the time.

Slip Leash: Essentially a leash with a collar built in, similar to what a dog-show handler uses to show a dog. This British-style collar has a ring on the end so that you can form a slip collar. Useful if you have to catch your own runaway dog or a stray.

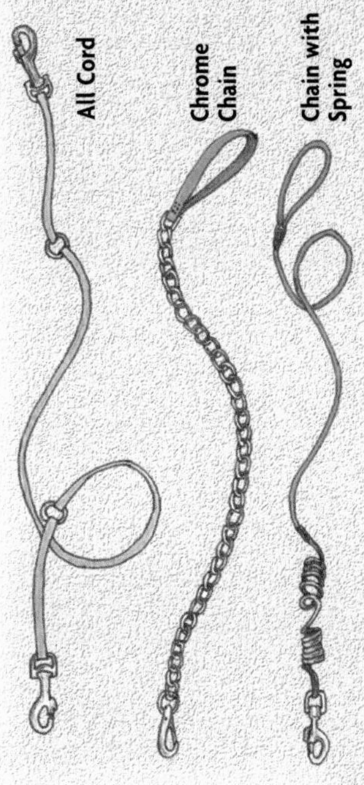

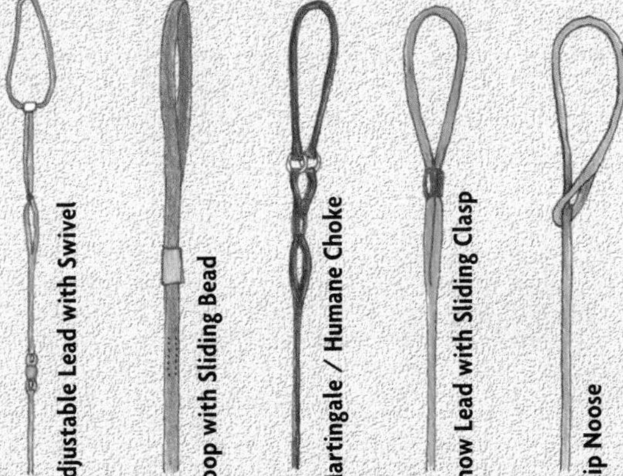

A Variety of Collar-and-Leash-in-One Products

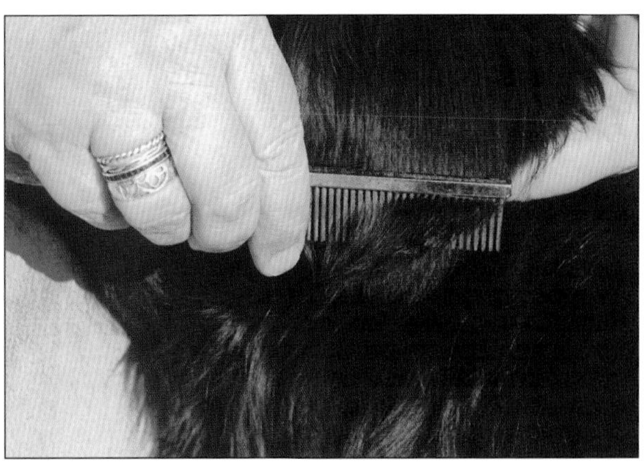

A metal comb is helpful for detangling the Flat-Coat's coat as the pup grows up and the hair grows longer.

consider purchasing a retractable lead. A retractable lead is excellent for walking adult dogs that are already leash-wise. This type of lead allows the dog to roam farther away from you and explore a wider area when out walking, and also retracts when you need to keep him close to you.

HOME SAFETY FOR YOUR PUPPY

The importance of puppy-proofing cannot be overstated. In addition to making your house comfortable for your Flat-Coated Retriever's arrival, you also must make sure that your house is safe for your puppy before you bring him home. There are countless hazards in the owner's personal living environment that a pup can sniff, chew, swallow or destroy. Many are obvious; others are not. Do a thorough advance house check to remove or rearrange those things that could hurt your puppy, keeping any potentially dangerous items out of areas to which he will have access.

Electrical cords are especially dangerous, since puppies view them as irresistible chew toys. Unplug and remove all exposed cords or fasten them beneath a baseboard where the puppy cannot reach them. Veterinarians and firefighters can tell you horror stories about electrical burns and house fires that resulted from puppy-chewed electrical cords. Consider this a most serious precaution for your puppy and the rest of your family.

Scout your home for tiny objects that might be seen at a pup's eye level. Keep medication

SWEETS THAT KILL

Antifreeze would be every dog's favorite topping for a chocolate sundae! However, antifreeze, just like chocolate, kills dogs. Ethylene glycol, found in antifreeze, causes acute renal failure in dogs and can be fatal. Dogs suffering from kidney failure expel little or no urine, act lethargical, may experience vomiting or diarrhea and may resist activity and drinking water. Just a single teaspoon of antifreeze is enough to kill a dog (depending on the size); even for large dogs, it takes only a tablespoon or two! Like that irresistible chocolate, antifreeze is sweet-tasting and smells yummy. Keep it away from your dog!

bottles and cleaning supplies well out of reach, and do the same with waste baskets and other trash containers. It goes without saying that you should not use rodent poison or other toxic chemicals in any puppy area and that you must keep such containers safely locked up. You will be amazed at how many places a curious puppy can discover!

Once your house has cleared inspection, check your yard. A sturdy fence, well embedded into the ground, will give your dog a safe place to play and potty. Although Flat-Coated Retrievers are not known to be climbers or fence jumpers, they are very athletic dogs, so a 6-foot-high fence is necessary to contain an agile youngster or adult. Check the fence periodically for necessary repairs. If there is a weak link or space to squeeze through, you can be sure a determined Flat-Coat will discover it.

The garage and shed can be hazardous places for a pup, as things like fertilizers, chemicals and tools are usually kept there. It's best to keep these areas off limits to the pup. Antifreeze is especially dangerous to dogs, as they find the taste appealing and it takes only a few licks from the driveway to kill a dog, puppy or adult, small breed or large.

TOXIC PLANTS

Plants are natural puppy magnets, but many can be harmful, even fatal, if ingested by a puppy or adult dog. Scout your yard and home interior and remove any plants, bushes or flowers that could be even mildly dangerous. It could save your puppy's life. You can obtain a complete list of toxic plants from your veterinarian, at the public library or by looking online.

Keep an eye on what your snooping Flat-Coat is up to so that you can make sure he doesn't follow his nose into trouble.

VISITING THE VETERINARIAN

A good veterinarian is your Flat-Coated Retriever puppy's best health insurance policy. If you do not already have a vet, ask friends and experienced dog people in your area for recommendations so that you can select a vet before you bring your Flat-Coat puppy home. Also arrange for your puppy's first veterinary examination beforehand, since many vets do not have appointments available immediately and your puppy should visit the vet within a day or so of coming home.

It's important to make sure your puppy's first visit to the vet is a pleasant and positive one. The vet should take great care to befriend the pup and handle him gently to make their first meeting a positive experience. The vet will give the pup a thorough physical examination and set up a schedule for vaccinations and other necessary wellness visits. Be sure to show your vet any health and inoculation records, which you should have received from your breeder. Your vet is a great source of canine health information, so be sure to ask questions and take notes. Creating a health journal for your puppy will make a handy reference for his wellness and any future health problems that may arise.

ASK THE VET

Help your vet help you to become a well-informed dog owner. Don't be shy about becoming involved in your puppy's veterinary care by asking questions and gaining as much knowledge as you can. For starters, ask what shots your puppy is getting and what diseases they prevent, and discuss with your vet the safest way to vaccinate. Find out what is involved in your dog's annual wellness visits. If you plan to spay or neuter, discuss the best age at which to have this done. Start out on the right "paw" with your puppy's vet and develop good communication with him, as he will care for your dog's health throughout the dog's entire life.

On the move! Along with chewing, another favorite pastime of Flat-Coat pups is exploring.

MEETING THE FAMILY

Your Flat-Coated Retriever's homecoming is an exciting time for all members of the family, and it's only natural that everyone will be eager to meet him, pet him and play with him. However, for the puppy's sake, it's best to make these initial family meetings as uneventful as possible so that the pup is not overwhelmed with too much too soon. Remember, he has just left his dam and his littermates and is away from the breeder's home for the first time. Despite his fuzzy wagging tail, he is still apprehensive and wondering where he is and who all these strange humans are. It's best to let him explore on his own and meet the family members as he feels comfortable. Let him investigate all the new smells, sights and sounds at his own pace. Children should be especially careful to not get overly excited, use loud voices or hug the pup too tightly. Be calm, gentle and affectionate, and be ready to comfort him if he appears frightened or uneasy.

Be sure to show your puppy his new crate during this first day home. Toss a treat or two inside the crate; if he associates the crate with food, he will associate the crate with good things. If he is comfortable with the crate, you can offer him his first meal inside it. Leave the door ajar so he can wander in and out as he chooses.

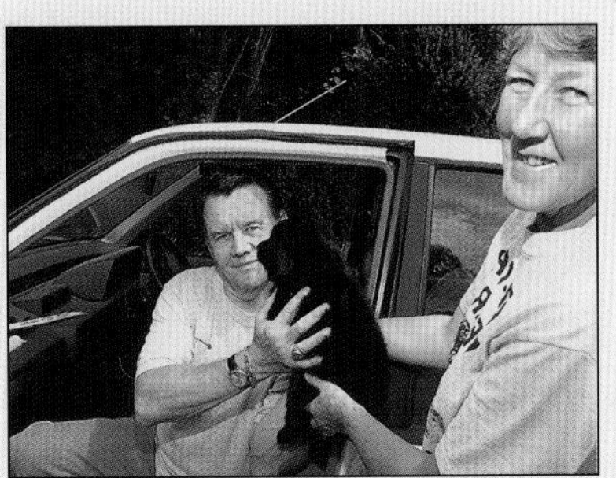

FIRST CAR RIDE

The ride to your home from the breeder will no doubt be your puppy's first automobile experience, and you should make every effort to keep him comfortable and secure. Bring a large towel or small blanket for the puppy to lie on during the trip and an extra towel in case the pup gets carsick or has a potty accident. It's best to have another person with you to hold the puppy in his lap. Most puppies will fall fast asleep from the rolling motion of the car. If the ride is lengthy, you may have to stop so that the puppy can relieve himself, so be sure to bring a leash and collar for those stops. Avoid rest areas for potty trips, since those are frequented by many dogs, who may carry parasites or disease. It's better to stop at grassy areas near gas stations or shopping centers to prevent unhealthy exposure for your pup.

FIRST NIGHT IN HIS NEW HOME

So much has happened in your Flat-Coated Retriever puppy's first day away from the breeder. He's had his first car ride to his new home. He's met his new human family and perhaps the other family pets. He has explored his new house and yard, at least those places where he is to be allowed during his

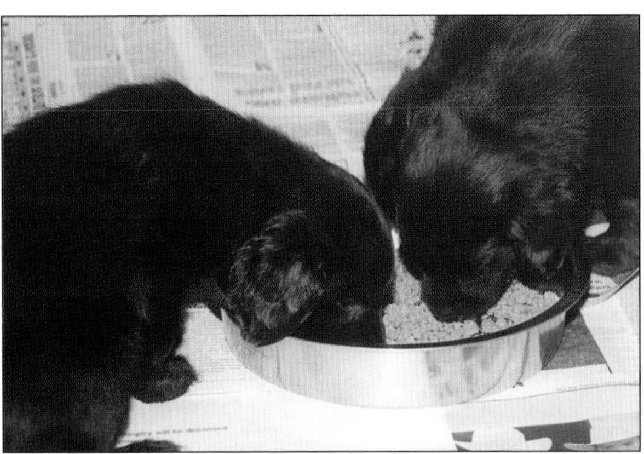

Puppies grow up doing everything together—playing, sleeping, eating, etc.—and will miss each other's company when they go to new homes.

first weeks at home. He may have visited his new veterinarian. He has eaten his first meal or two away from his dam and littermates. Surely that's enough to tire out an eight-week-old Flat-Coated Retriever pup…or so you hope!

It's bedtime. During the day, the pup investigated his crate, which is his new den and sleeping space, so it is not entirely strange to him. Line the crate with a soft towel or blanket that he can snuggle into and gently place him into the crate for the night. Some breeders send home a piece of bedding from where the pup slept with his littermates, and those familiar scents are a great comfort for the puppy on his first night without his siblings.

He will probably whine or cry. The puppy is objecting to the confinement and the fact that he is alone for the first time. This can be a stressful time for you as well as for the pup. It's important that you remain strong and don't let the puppy out of his crate to comfort him. He will fall asleep eventually. If you release him, the puppy will learn that crying means "out" and will continue that habit. You are laying the groundwork for future habits. Some breeders find that soft music can soothe a crying pup and help him get to sleep; others recommend placing the crate in your bedroom at night for the first few weeks to help make your pup feel secure and further your bond. However, don't give into his

THE FAMILY FELINE

A resident cat has feline squatter's rights. The cat will treat the newcomer (your puppy) as she sees fit, regardless of what you do or say. So it's best to let the two of them work things out on their own terms. Cats have a height advantage and will generally leap to higher ground to avoid direct contact with a rambunctious pup. Some will hiss and boldly swat at a pup who passes by or tries to reach the cat. Keep the puppy under control in the presence of the cat and they will eventually become accustomed to each other.

Here's a hint: move the cat's litter box where the puppy can't get into it! It's best to do so well before the pup comes home so the cat is used to the new location.

whining and let him sleep on the bed with you.

SOCIALIZING YOUR PUPPY

The first 20 weeks of your Flat-Coated Retriever puppy's life are the most important of his entire lifetime. A properly socialized puppy will grow up to be a confident and stable adult who will be a pleasure to live with and a welcome addition to the neighborhood.

The importance of socialization cannot be overemphasized. Research on canine behavior has proven that puppies who are not exposed to new sights, sounds, people and animals during their first 20 weeks of life will grow up to be timid and fearful, even aggressive, and unable to flourish outside of their familiar home environment.

Socializing your puppy is not difficult and, in fact, will be a fun time for you both. Lead training goes hand in hand with socialization, so your puppy will be learning how to walk on a lead at the same time that he's meeting the neighborhood. Because the Flat-Coated Retriever is such a terrific breed, your puppy will enjoy being "the new kid on the block." Take him for short walks, to the park and to other dog-friendly places where he will encounter new people, especially children. Puppies automatically recognize children as "little people" and are drawn to play with them. Just make sure that you supervise these meetings and that the children do not get too rough or encourage him to play too hard. An overzealous pup can often nip too hard, frightening the child and in turn making the puppy overly excited. A bad experience in puppyhood can impact a dog for life, so a pup that has a negative experience with a child may grow up to be shy or even aggressive around children.

Take your puppy along on your daily errands. Puppies are natural "people magnets," and most people who see your pup will want to pet him. All of these encounters will help to mold him

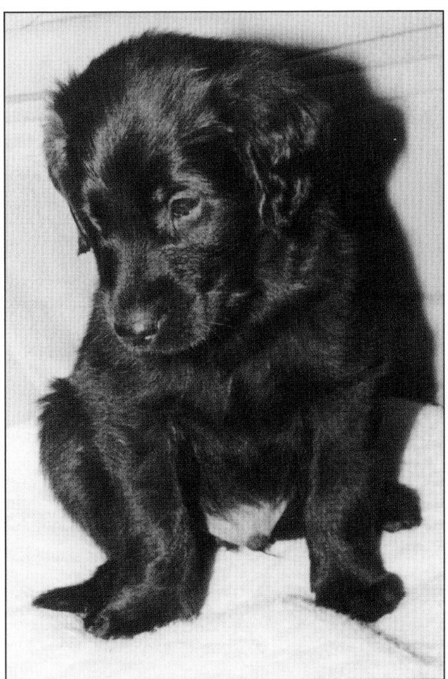

A young Flat-Coat puppy, ready for a bright future ahead!

Puppy kisses and affection make all the work you put into raising him worthwhile!

into a confident adult dog. Likewise, you will soon feel like a confident, responsible dog owner, rightly proud of your handsome Flat-Coated Retriever.

Be especially careful of your puppy's encounters and experiences during the eight-to-ten-week-old period, which is also called the "fear period." This is a serious imprinting period, and all contact during this time should be gentle and positive. A frightening or negative event could leave a permanent impression that could affect his future behavior if a similar situation arises.

Also make sure that your puppy has received his first and second rounds of vaccinations before you expose him to other dogs or bring him to places that other dogs may frequent. Avoid dog parks and other strange-dog areas until your vet assures you that your puppy is fully immunized and resistant to the diseases that can be passed between canines. Discuss socialization with your breeder, as some breeders recommend socializing the puppy even before he has received all of his inoculations, depending on how outgoing the puppy may be.

LEADER OF THE PUPPY'S PACK

Like other canines, your puppy needs an authority figure, someone he can look up to and regard as the leader of his "pack." His first pack leader was his dam, who taught him to be polite and not chew too hard on her ears or nip at her muzzle. He learned those same lessons from his littermates. If he played too rough, they cried in pain and stopped the game, which sent an important message to the rowdy puppy.

As puppies play together, they are also struggling to

BE CONSISTENT

Consistency is a key element, in fact is absolutely necessary, to a puppy's learning environment. A behavior (such as chewing, jumping up or climbing onto the furniture) cannot be forbidden one day and then allowed the next. That will only confuse the pup, and he will not understand what he is supposed to do. Just one or two episodes of allowing an undesirable behavior to "slide" will imprint that behavior on a puppy's brain and make that behavior more difficult to erase or change.

determine who will be the boss. Being pack animals, dogs need someone to be in charge. If a litter of puppies remained together beyond puppyhood, one of the pups would emerge as the strongest one, the one who calls the shots.

Once your puppy leaves the pack, he will look intuitively for a new leader. If he does not recognize you as that leader, he will try to assume that position for himself. Of course, it is hard to imagine your adorable Flat-Coated Retriever puppy trying to be in charge when he is so small and seemingly helpless. You must remember that these are natural canine instincts. Do not cave in and allow your pup to get the upper "paw"!

Just as socialization is so important during these first 20 weeks, so too is your puppy's early education. He was born without any bad habits. He does not know what is good or bad behavior. If he does things like nipping and digging, it's because he is having fun and doesn't know that humans consider these things as "bad." It's your job to teach him proper puppy manners, and this is the best time to accomplish that…before he has developed bad habits, since it is much more difficult to "unlearn" or correct unacceptable learned behavior than to teach good behavior from the start.

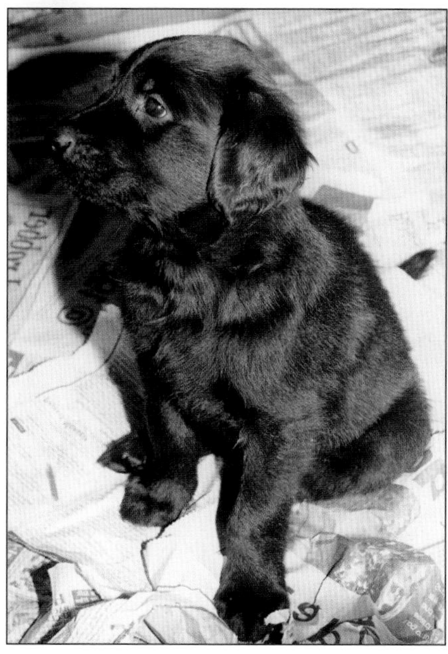

At such a young age, a pup does not get to see much of the outside world. He receives most of his early socialization from his dam, his littermates and his breeder.

Make sure that all members of the family understand the importance of being consistent when training their new puppy. If you tell the puppy to stay off the sofa and your daughter allows him to cuddle on the couch with her to watch her favorite television show, your pup will be confused about what he is and is not allowed to do. Have a family conference before your pup comes home so that everyone understands the basic principles of puppy training and the rules you have set forth for the pup, and agrees to follow them.

The old adage that "an ounce of prevention is worth a pound of cure" is especially true when it comes to puppies. It is much easier to prevent inappropriate behavior than it is to change it. It's also easier and less stressful for the pup, since it will keep discipline to a minimum and create a more positive learning environment for him. That, in turn, will also be easier on you!

Here are a few commonsense tips to keep your belongings safe and your puppy out of trouble:

- Keep your closet doors closed and your shoes, socks and other apparel off the floor so your puppy can't get at them.
- Keep a secure lid on the trash container or put the trash where your puppy can't dig into it. He can't damage what he can't reach!
- Supervise your puppy at all times to make sure he is not getting into mischief. If he starts to chew the corner of the rug, you can distract him instantly by tossing a toy for him to fetch. You also will be able to whisk him outside when you notice that he is about to piddle on the carpet. If you can't see your puppy, you can't teach him or correct his behavior.

SOLVING PUPPY PROBLEMS

Chewing and Nipping

Nipping at fingers and toes is normal puppy behavior. Chewing is also the way that puppies investigate their surroundings. However, you will have to teach your puppy that chewing anything other than his toys is not acceptable. That won't happen overnight and at times puppy teeth will test your patience. Remember that it's natural for a Flat-Coat to want something in his mouth, so you must direct his oral tendencies onto appropriate objects. If you allow nipping on you and chewing on forbidden items to continue, just think about the damage that a mature Flat-Coated Retriever can do with a full set of adult teeth.

Whenever your puppy nips your hand or fingers, cry out "Ouch!" in a loud voice, which should startle your puppy and stop him from nipping, even if only for a moment. Immediately distract him by offering a small treat or an appropriate toy for him to chew instead (which means having chew toys and puppy treats handy or in your pockets at all times). Praise him when he takes the toy and tell him what a good fellow he is. Praise is even more important in puppy training as discipline and correction.

Puppies also tend to nip at children more often than adults, since they perceive little ones to be more vulnerable and more similar to their littermates. Teach your children appropriate responses to nipping behavior. If they are unable to handle it themselves, you may have to intervene. Puppy nips can be quite painful and a child's frightened reaction will only encourage a puppy to nip harder, which is a natural canine response. As with all other puppy situations, interaction between your Flat-Coated Retriever puppy and children should be supervised.

Chewing on objects, not just family members' fingers and ankles, is also normal canine behavior that can be especially tedious (for the owner, not the pup) during the teething period when the puppy's adult teeth are coming in. At this stage, chewing just plain feels good. Furniture legs and cabinet corners are common puppy favorites. Shoes and other personal items also taste pretty good to a pup.

The best solution is, once again, prevention. If you value something, keep it tucked away and out of reach. You can't hide your dining-room table in a closet, but you can try to deflect the chewing by applying a bitter product made just to deter dogs from chewing. Available in a spray or cream, this substance is vile-tasting, although safe for dogs, and most puppies will avoid the forbidden object after one tiny taste. You also can apply the product to your leather leash if the puppy tries to chew on his lead during leash-training sessions.

Keep a ready supply of safe chews handy to offer your Flat-Coated Retriever as a distraction when he starts to chew on something that's a "no-no." Give him a toy to carry around. Remember, at this tender age, he does not yet know what is permitted or forbidden, so you have to be "on call" every minute he's awake and on the prowl.

You may lose a treasure or two during puppy's growing-up period, and the furniture could sustain a nasty nick or two. These can be trying times, so be prepared for those inevitable accidents and comfort yourself in knowing that this too shall pass.

TEETHING TIME

All puppies chew. It's normal canine behavior. Chewing just plain feels good to a puppy, especially during the three- to five-month teething period when the adult teeth are breaking through the gums. Rather than attempting to eliminate such a strong natural chewing instinct, you will be more successful if you redirect it and teach your puppy what he may or may not chew. Correct inappropriate chewing with a sharp "No!" and offer him a chew toy, praising him when he takes it. Don't become discouraged. Chewing usually decreases after the adult teeth have come in.

Jumping Up

Flat-Coats are exuberant dogs as youngsters and adults, often showing their enthusiasm by jumping up...on you, your guests, your counters and your furniture. Just another normal part of growing up, and one you need to meet head-on before it becomes an ingrained habit.

The key to jump correction is consistency. You cannot correct your Flat-Coat for jumping up on you today, then allow it to happen tomorrow by greeting him with hugs and kisses. As you have learned by now, consistency is critical to all puppy lessons. For starters, try turning your back as soon as the puppy jumps. Jumping up is a means of gaining your attention and, if the pup can't see your face, he may get discouraged and learn that he loses eye contact with his beloved master when he jumps up.

Leash corrections also work, and most puppies respond well to a leash tug if they jump. Grasp the leash close to the puppy's collar and give a quick tug downward, using the command "Off." Do not use the word "Down," since "Down" is used to teach the puppy to lie down, which is a separate action that he will learn during his education in the basic commands. As soon as the puppy has backed off, tell him to sit and immediately praise him for doing so. This will take many repetitions and won't be accomplished quickly, so don't get discouraged or give up; you must be even more persistent than your puppy.

Another method used for jump correction is the spritzer bottle. Fill a spray bottle with water mixed with a bit of lemon juice or vinegar. As soon as puppy jumps, command him "Off" and spritz him with the water mixture. Of course, that means having the spray bottle handy whenever or wherever jumping usually occurs.

Yet another method to discourage jumping is grasping the puppy's paws and holding them gently but firmly until he struggles to get away. Wait a brief moment or two, then release his paws and give him a command to sit. He should soon learn that jumping gets him into an uncomfortable predicament.

Children are major victims of puppy jumping, since puppies view little people as ready targets for jumping up as well as nipping. If your children (or their friends) are unable to dispense jump corrections, you will have to intervene and handle it for them.

Important to prevention is also knowing what you should not do. Never kick your Flat-Coat (for any reason, not just for jumping) or knock him in the chest with your knee. That maneuver could actually harm your puppy. Vets can tell you stories about puppies who suffered broken bones after being banged about when they jumped up.

PROPER CARE OF YOUR

FLAT-COATED RETRIEVER

Adding a Flat-Coated Retriever to your household means adding a new family member who will need your care each and every day. When your Flat-Coated Retriever pup first comes home, you will start a routine with him so that, as he grows up, your dog will have a daily schedule just as you do. The aspects of your dog's daily care will likewise become regular parts of your day, so you'll both have a new schedule. Dogs learn by consistency and thrive on routine: regular times for meals, exercise, grooming and potty trips are just as important for your dog as they are for you! Your dog's schedule will depend much on your family's daily routine, but remember that you now have a new member of the family who is part of your day every day.

NOT HUNGRY?

No dog in his right mind would turn down his dinner, would he? If you notice that your dog has lost interest in his food, there could be any number of causes. Dental problems are a common cause of appetite loss, one that is often overlooked. If your dog has a toothache, a loose tooth or sore gums from infection, chances are it doesn't feel so good to chew. Think about when you've had a toothache! If your dog does not approach the food bowl with his usual enthusiasm, look inside his mouth for signs of a problem. Whatever the cause, you'll want to consult your vet so that your chow hound can get back to his happy, hungry self as soon as possible.

FEEDING

Feeding your dog the best diet is based on various factors, including age, activity level, overall condition and size of breed. When you visit the breeder, he will share with you his advice about the proper diet for your Flat-Coat based on his experience with the breed and the foods with which he has had success. Likewise, your vet will be a helpful source of advice throughout the dog's life and will aid you in planning a diet for optimal health.

FEEDING THE PUPPY

Of course, your pup's very first food will be his dam's milk. There may be special situations in which pups fail to nurse, necessitating that the breeder hand-feed them with a formula, but for the most part pups spend the first weeks of life nursing from their dam. The breeder weans the pups by gradually introducing solid foods and decreasing the milk meals. Pups may even start themselves off on the weaning process, albeit inadvertently, if they snatch bites from their mom's food bowl.

By the time the pups are ready for new homes, they are fully weaned and eating a good puppy food. As a new owner, you may be thinking, "Great! The breeder has taken care of the hard part." Not so fast.

A puppy's first year of life is the time when all or most of his growth and development takes place, although a Flat-Coat continues to mature physically well past his first birthday. This growth period is a delicate time, and diet plays a huge role in proper skeletal and muscular formation. Improper diet and exercise habits can lead to damaging problems that will compromise the dog's health and movement for his entire life. That being said, new owners should not worry needlessly. With the myriad types of food formulated specifically for growing pups of different-sized breeds, dog-food manufacturers have taken much of the guesswork out of feeding your puppy for healthy growth. Since puppy formulas are designed to provide the nutrition that a growing puppy needs, it is

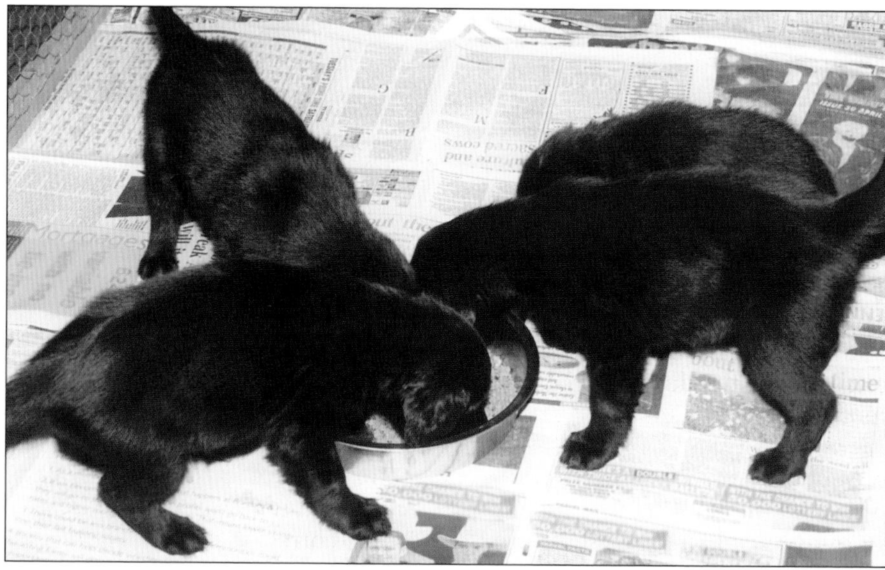

The breeder starts the pups on good solid food and will be a helpful source of advice about appropriate dietary changes as your pup grows.

unnecessary and, in fact, can prove harmful to add supplements to the diet. Research has shown that too much of certain vitamin supplements and minerals predispose a dog to skeletal problems. It's by no means a case of "if a little is good, a lot is better." At every stage of your dog's life, too much or too little in the way of nutrients can be harmful, which is why a manufactured complete food is the easiest way to know that your dog is getting what he needs.

Because of a young pup's small body and accordingly small digestive system, his daily portion will be divided up into small meals throughout the day. This can mean starting off with three or more meals a day and decreasing the number of meals as the pup matures. It is generally thought that dividing the day's food into two meals on a morning/evening schedule is healthier for the dog's digestion and for bloat prevention (bloat/gastric torsion is discussed in detail in the health chapter).

Regarding the feeding schedule, feeding the pup at the same times and in the same place each day is important for both housebreaking purposes and establishing the dog's everyday routine. As for the amount to feed, growing puppies generally need proportionately more food per body weight than their adult counterparts, but a pup should never be allowed to gain excess weight. Dogs of all ages should be kept in proper body condition, but extra weight can strain a pup's developing frame, causing skeletal problems.

Your dog's dietary needs will vary depending on his activity level. A working or especially active Flat-Coat will have a higher caloric requirement than one with a more sedentary life.

Watch your pup's weight as he grows and, if the recommended amounts seem to be too much or too little for your pup, consult the vet about appropriate dietary changes. Keep in mind that treats, although small, can quickly add up throughout the day, contributing unnecessary calories. Treats are fine when used prudently; opt for dog treats specially formulated to be healthy or for nutritious snacks like small pieces of cheese or cooked chicken.

Feeding the Adult Dog

For the adult (meaning physically mature) dog, feeding properly is about maintenance, not growth. Again, correct weight is a concern.

Treats can be used as rewards in training, but don't overdo it. Too many treats can spoil the balanced nutrition that your Flat-Coat gets from his complete food.

Your dog should appear fit and should have an evident "waist." His ribs should not be protruding (a sign of being underweight), but they should be covered by only a slight layer of fat. Under normal circumstances, an adult dog can be maintained fairly easily with a high-quality nutritionally complete adult-formula food.

Factor treats into your dog's overall daily caloric intake, and avoid offering table scraps. Overweight dogs are more prone to health problems, and some "people foods," like chocolate, onions, grapes, raisins and nuts, are toxic to dogs. Research has shown that obesity takes years off a dog's life. With that in mind, resist the urge to overfeed and over-treat. Don't make unnecessary additions to your dog's diet, whether with tidbits or with extra vitamins and minerals.

The amount of food needed for proper maintenance will vary depending on the individual dog's activity level, but you will be able to tell whether the daily portions are keeping him in good shape. With the wide variety of good complete foods available, choosing what to feed is largely a matter of personal preference. Just as with the puppy, the adult dog should have consistency in his mealtimes and feeding place, being sure to allow at least two hours before and after mealtimes until your Flat-Coat is permitted to exercise. In addition to a consistent routine, regular mealtimes also allow the owner to see how much his dog his eating. If the dog seems never to be satisfied or, likewise, becomes uninterested in his food, the owner will know right away that something is wrong and can consult the vet.

Diets for the Aging Dog

A good rule of thumb is that once a dog has reached 75% of his expected lifespan, he has reached "senior citizen" or geriatric status. Your Flat-Coated Retriever will be considered a senior at about 7 years of age; based on size and breed-specific factors, he has a projected lifespan of about 10–12 years. (The smallest breeds generally enjoy the longest lives and the largest breeds the shortest.)

What does aging have to do

with your dog's diet? No, he won't get a discount at the local diner's early-bird special. Yes, he will require some dietary changes to accommodate the changes that come along with increased age. One change is that the older dog's dietary needs become more similar to that of a puppy. Specifically, dogs can metabolize more protein as youngsters and seniors than in the adult-maintenance stage. Discuss with your vet whether you need to switch to a higher-protein or senior-formulated food or whether your current adult-dog food contains sufficient nutrition for the senior.

Watching the dog's weight remains essential, even more so in the senior stage. Older dogs are already more vulnerable to illness, and obesity only contributes to their susceptibility to problems. As the older dog becomes less active and thus exercises less, his regular portions may cause him to gain weight. At this point, you may consider decreasing his daily food intake or switching to a reduced-calorie food. As with other changes, you should consult your vet for advice.

Don't Forget the Water!

Regardless of what type of food he eats, there's no doubt that your Flat-Coat needs plenty of water. Fresh cold water, in a clean bowl, should be made available to your dog. There are special circumstances, such as during puppy

Water is an essential part of a dog's diet at any age. Breeders often use dispensers that attach to the crate or pen to supply their litters with water.

housebreaking, when you will want to monitor your pup's water intake so that you will be able to predict when he will need to relieve himself, but water must be available to him nonetheless. Water is essential for hydration and proper body function just as it is in humans.

You will get to know how much your dog typically drinks in a day. Of course, in the heat or if exercising vigorously, he will be more thirsty and will drink more. However, if he begins to drink noticeably more water for no apparent reason, this could signal any of various problems, and you are advised to consult your vet.

A word of caution concerning your deep-chested dog's water intake: he should never be allowed to gulp water, especially at mealtimes. In fact, his water intake should be limited at mealtimes as a rule. This simple daily precaution can go a long way in protecting your dog from the dangerous and potentially fatal gastric torsion (bloat).

EXERCISE

We all know the importance of exercise for humans, so it should come as no surprise that it is essential for our canine friends as well. Now, regardless of your own level of fitness, get ready to assume the role of personal trainer for your dog. It's not as hard as it sounds, and it will have health benefits for you, too.

Just as with anything else you do with your dog, you must set a routine for his exercise. It's the same as your daily morning run before work or never missing the 7 p.m. aerobics class. If you plan it and get into the habit of actually doing it, it will become just another part of your day. Think of it as making daily exercise appointments with your dog, and stick to your schedule.

The Flat-Coat is a sporting dog with an abundance of energy and enthusiasm. Dogs with health or orthopedic problems may have specific limitations, so their exercise plans are best devised with the help of a vet. For healthy dogs, there are many ways to fit activity for your Flat-Coat into your day. Depending on your schedule, you may plan a walk or activity session in the morning and again in the evening, or do it all in one long session each day. Again, you should plan exercise sessions at least two hours away from mealtimes (before and after). Walking is the most popular way to exercise a dog (it's good for you, too!); other suggestions include retrieving games (of course!), jogging and disc-catching or other interactive games. If you have a safe body of water nearby, swimming is a natural form of exercise for Flat-Coats, putting no stress on his frame and thoroughly enjoyed.

Some precautions should be taken with a puppy's exercise. During his first year, when he is doing most of his growing and developing, your Flat-Coated Retriever should not be subjected to stressful activity that stresses his body (e.g., jumping, too-long walks, jogging). Short walks at a comfortable pace and play sessions in the yard are good for a growing pup, and his exercise can be increased as he grows up.

For overweight dogs, dietary changes and activity will help the goal of weight loss. (Sound familiar?) While they should of course be encouraged to be active, remember not to overdo it, as the excess weight is already putting strain on his vital organs and bones. As for highly active dogs, some of them never seem to tire! They will enjoy time spent with their owners, doing things together.

Regardless of your dog's condition and activity level, exercise offers benefits to all dogs and owners. Consider the fact that dogs who are kept active are more stimulated both physically and mentally, meaning that they are less likely to become bored and lapse into destructive behavior. Also consider the benefits of one-on-one time with your dog every day, continually strengthening the bond between the two of you. Furthermore, exercising together will improve health and longevity for both of you. You both need exercise, and now you and your dog have a workout partner and motivator!

GROOMING

BRUSHING

A pin brush and a comb with both narrow- and wide-spaced teeth are good for regular coat maintenance. Get in a routine of brushing and combing your Flat-Coat a few times weekly. Brushing is effective for removing dead hair, keeping the coat free of mats and tangles and stimulating the dog's natural oils to add shine and a healthy look to the coat. Regular grooming sessions are also a good way to spend time with your dog and will help to minimize the dog's hair being shed all over your house. Many dogs like the feel of being brushed and will enjoy the routine.

A comb or comb-like device is used to remove tangles and debris from the longer hair on the Flat-Coat's tail.

Bathing

In general, dogs need to be bathed only a few times a year, possibly more often if your dog gets into something messy or if he starts to smell like a dog. Show dogs are usually bathed more frequently, although this depends on the owner and the show schedule. Bathing too frequently can have negative effects on the Flat-Coat's skin and coat, removing its natural oils and water-repellent qualities, and causing dryness.

If you give your dog his first bath when he is young, he will become accustomed to the process. Wrestling a dog into the tub or chasing a freshly shampooed dog who has escaped from the bath will be no fun! Fortunately for Flat-Coat owners, their dogs are natural water lovers.

Before bathing the dog, have the items you'll need close at hand. First decide where you will bathe the dog. You should have a tub or basin with a non-slip surface. In warm weather, some like to use a portable pool in the yard, although you'll want to make sure your dog doesn't head for the nearest dirt pile following his bath! You will also need a hose or shower spray to wet the coat thoroughly, a shampoo formulated for dogs, absorbent towels and perhaps a blow dryer. Human shampoos are too harsh for dogs' coats and will dry them out.

Before wetting the dog, give him a brush-through to remove

WATER SHORTAGE

No matter how well behaved your dog is, bathing is always a project! Nothing can substitute for a good warm bath, but owners do have the option of giving their dogs "dry" baths. Pet shops sell excellent products, in both powder and spray forms, designed for spot-cleaning your dog. These dry shampoos are convenient for touch-up jobs when you don't have the time to bathe your dog in the traditional way.

Muddy feet, messy behinds and smelly coats can be spot-cleaned and deodorized with a "wet-nap"-style cleaner. On those days when your dog insists on rolling in fresh goose droppings and there's no time for a bath, a spot bath can save the day. These pre-moistened wipes are also handy for other grooming needs like wiping faces, ears and eyes and freshening tails and behinds.

Weather permitting, outdoor bathing of your Flat-Coated Retriever can be fun. The dogs enjoy the water, and it eliminates much of the cleanup indoors.

any dead hair, dirt and mats. Make sure he is at ease in the tub and have the water at a comfortable temperature. Begin bathing by wetting the coat all the way down to the skin. Massage in the shampoo, keeping it away from his face and eyes. Rinse him thoroughly, again avoiding the eyes and ears, as you don't want to get water into the ear canals. A thorough rinsing is important, as shampoo residue is drying and itchy to the dog. After rinsing, wrap him in a towel to absorb the initial moisture. You can finish drying with either a towel or a blow dryer on low heat, held at a safe distance from the dog. You should keep the dog indoors and away from drafts until he is completely dry.

Nail Clipping

Having his nails trimmed is not on many dogs' lists of favorite things to do. With this in mind, you will need to accustom your puppy to the procedure at a young age so that he will sit still (well, as still as he can) for his pedicures. Long nails can cause the dog's feet to spread, which is not good for him; likewise, long nails can hurt if they unintentionally scratch, not good for you!

Some dogs' nails are worn down naturally by regular walking on hard surfaces, so the frequency with which you clip depends on your individual dog. Look at his

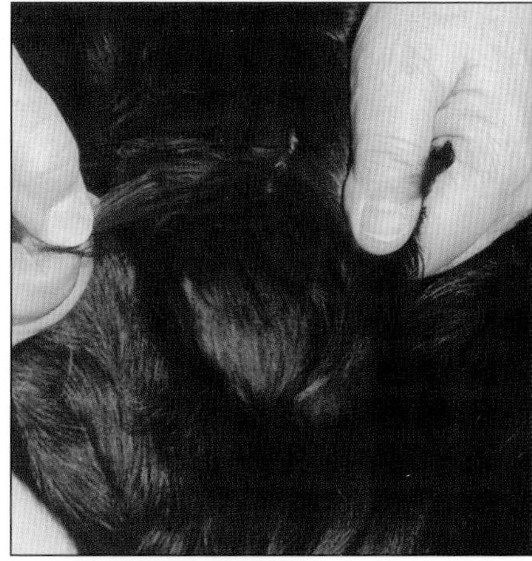

The feathering on the Flat-Coat's ears should be kept free of tangles and mats as part of your routine grooming.

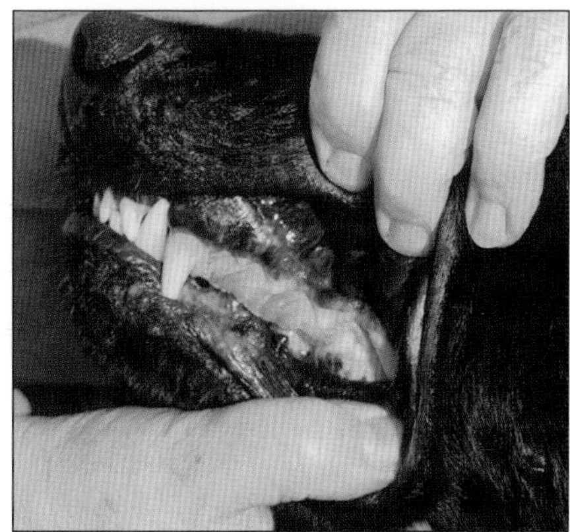

Brush your dog's teeth and examine his mouth on a regular basis. Report any changes or abnormalities to your vet.

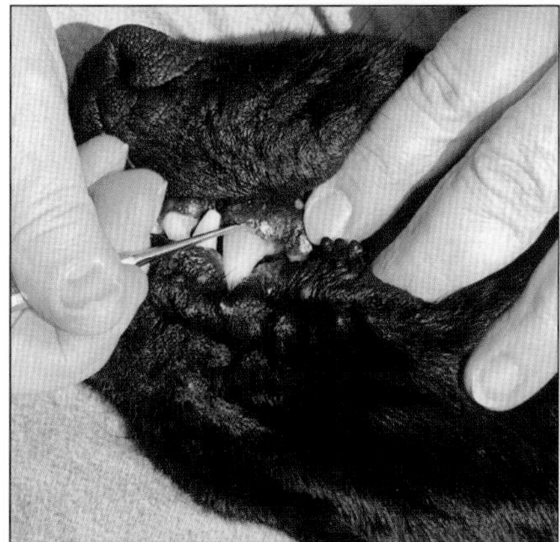

Scraping of the dog's teeth is best done by the vet. Sometimes this requires the dog to be anesthetized.

nails from time to time and clip as needed; a good way to know when it's time for a trim is if you hear your dog clicking as he walks across the floor.

There are several types of nail clippers and even electric nail-grinding tools made for dogs; first we'll discuss using the clipper. To start, have your clipper ready and some doggie treats on hand. You want your pup to view his nail-clipping sessions in a positive light, and what better way to convince him than with food? You may want to enlist the help of an assistant to comfort the pup and offer treats as you concentrate on the clipping itself. The guillotine-type clipper is thought of by many as the easiest type to use; the nail tip is inserted into the opening, and blades on the top and bottom snip it off in one clip.

Start by grasping the pup's paw; a little pressure on the foot pad causes the nail to extend, making it easier to clip. Clip off a little at a time. If you can see the "quick," which is a blood vessel that runs through each nail, you will know how much to trim, as you do not want to cut into the quick. On that note, if you do cut the quick, which will cause bleeding, you can stem the flow of blood with a styptic pencil or other clotting agent. If you mistakenly nip the quick, do not panic or fuss, as this will cause the pup to be afraid. Simply reassure the

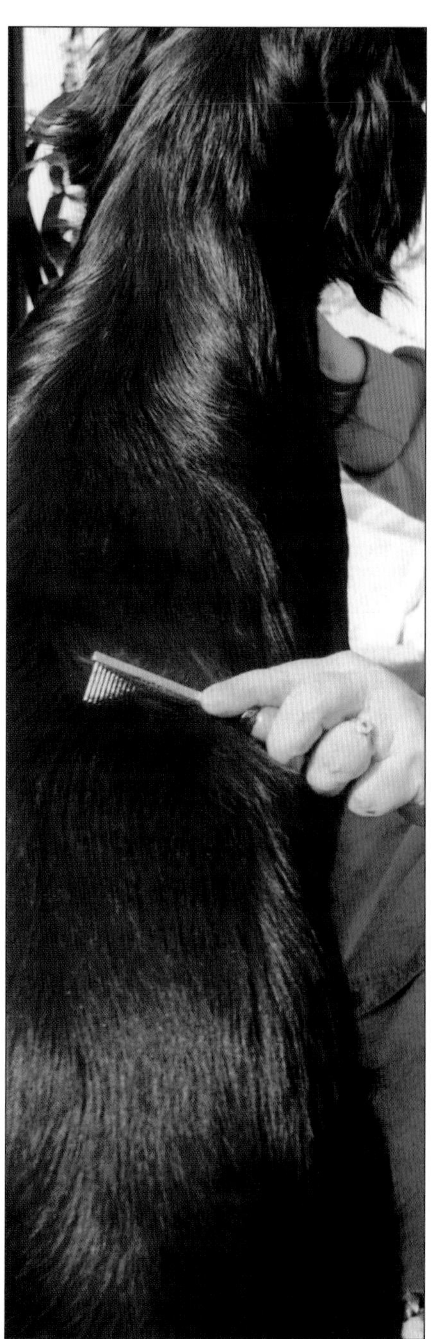

The Flat-Coat is a naturally beautiful breed that needs attention to his coat, but nothing fancy. You should tend to your dog's coat on a regular basis in order to keep it looking its best.

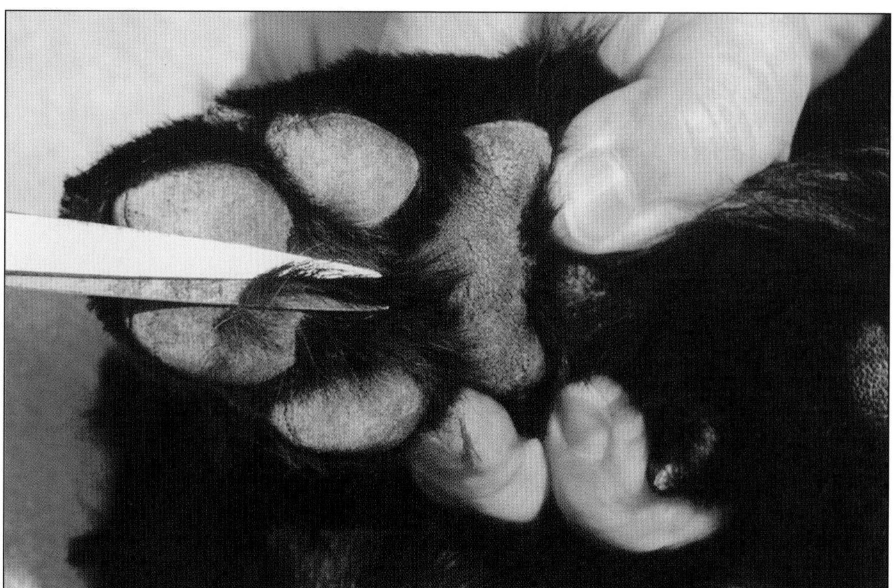

Excess hair growing on the bottom of the dog's feet between the pads should be trimmed to keep it comfortable for the dog.

pup, stop the bleeding and move on to the next nail. Don't be discouraged; you will become a professional canine pedicurist with practice.

You may or may not be able to see the quick, so it's best to just clip off a small bit at a time. If you see a dark dot in the center of the nail, this is the quick and your cue to stop clipping. Tell the puppy he's a "good boy" and offer a piece of treat with each nail. You can also use nail-clipping time to examine the footpads, making sure that they are not dry and cracked and that nothing has become embedded in them.

The nail grinder, the other choice, is many owners' first choice. Accustoming the puppy to the sound of the grinder and sensation of the buzz presents fewer challenges than the clipper, and there's no chance of cutting through the quick. Use the grinder on a low setting and always talk soothingly to your dog. He won't mind his salon visit, and he'll have nicely polished nails as well.

Ear Cleaning

While keeping your dog's ears clean unfortunately will not cause him to "hear" your commands any better, it will protect him from ear infection and ear-mite infestation. In addition, a dog's ears are vulnerable to waxy build-up and to collecting foreign matter from the outdoors. Look in your dog's ears regularly to ensure that they look pink, clean and otherwise healthy. Even if they look fine, an odor in the ears signals a problem and means it's time to call the vet. The Flat-Coat's drop ears make him more prone to ear infections than prick-eared breeds; further, water left in the ears after swimming and other factors can contribute to ear infections in the breed.

A dog's ears should be cleaned regularly; once a week is suggested. Drying the ears after a swim is also recommended. Using a cotton ball or pad and never probing into the ear canal, wipe the ear gently. You can use an ear-cleansing liquid or powder available from your vet or pet-supply store; alternatively, you might prefer to use home-made solutions with ingredients like one part white vinegar and one part hydrogen peroxide. Ask your vet about home remedies before you attempt to concoct something on your own!

Keep your dog's ears free of excess hair by plucking it as needed. If done gently, this will be painless for the dog. Look for wax, brown droppings (a sign of ear mites), redness or any other abnormalities. At the first sign of a problem, contact your vet so that he can prescribe an appropriate medication.

Eye Care

During grooming sessions, pay extra attention to the condition of your dog's eyes. If the area around the eyes is soiled or if tear staining has occurred, there are various cleaning agents made especially for this purpose. Look at the dog's eyes to make sure no debris has entered; dogs who spend a lot of time outdoors are especially prone to this.

The signs of an eye infection are obvious: mucus, redness, puffiness, scabs or other signs of irritation. If your dog's eyes become infected, the vet will likely prescribe an antibiotic ointment for treatment. If you notice signs of more serious problems, such as opacities in the eyes, which usually indicate cataracts, consult the vet at once. Taking time to pay attention to your dog's eyes will alert you in the early stages of any problem so that you can get your dog treatment as soon as possible. You could save your dog's sight!

ID FOR YOUR DOG

You love your Flat-Coated Retriever and want to keep him safe. Of course, you take every precaution to prevent his escaping from the yard or becoming lost or stolen. You have a sturdy high fence and you always keep your dog on-lead when out and about in public places. If your dog is not properly identified, however, you are overlooking a major aspect of his safety. We hope to never be in a situation where our dog is missing, but we should practice prevention in the unfortunate case that this happens; identification greatly increases the chances of your dog's being returned to you.

There are several ways to identify your dog. First, the traditional dog tag should be a staple in your dog's wardrobe, attached to his everyday collar. Tags can be made of sturdy plastic and various metals and should include your contact information so that a person who finds the dog can get in touch with you right away to arrange his return. Many people today enjoy the wide range of decorative tags available, so have fun and create a tag to match your dog's personality. Of course, it is important that the tag stays on the collar, so have a secure "O" ring attachment; you also can explore the type of tag that slides right onto the collar.

In addition to the ID tag, which every dog should wear even if identified by another method, two other forms of identification have become popular: microchipping and tattooing. In microchipping, a tiny scannable chip is painlessly inserted under the dog's skin. The number is registered to you so that, if your lost dog turns up at a clinic or shelter, the chip can be scanned to retrieve your contact information.

The advantage of the microchip is that it is a permanent form of ID, but there are some factors to consider. Several different companies make microchips, and not all are compatible with the others' scanning devices. It's best to find a company with a universal microchip that can be read by scanners made by other companies as well. It won't do any good to have the dog chipped if the information cannot be retrieved. Also, not every humane society, shelter and clinic is equipped with a scanner, although more and more facilities are equipping themselves. In fact, many shelters microchip dogs that they adopt out to new homes.

In the US, there are five or six major microchip manufacturers as well as a few databases. The American Kennel Club's Companion Animal Recovery unit

The Flat-Coat is a happy, affectionate dog who will enjoy the attention you give him in ensuring his safety and well-being.

PET OR STRAY?

Besides the obvious benefit of providing your contact information to whoever finds your lost dog, an ID tag makes your dog more approachable and more likely to be recovered. A strange dog wandering the neighborhood without a collar and tags will look like a stray, while the collar and tags indicate that the dog is someone's pet. Even if the ID tags become detached from the collar, the collar alone will make a person more likely to pick up the dog.

works in conjunction with HomeAgain™ Companion Animal Retrieval System (Schering-Plough). In the UK, The Kennel Club is affiliated with the National Pet Register, operated by Wood Green Animal Shelters.

Humane societies and veterinary clinics offer microchipping service, which is usually very affordable. Because the microchip is not visible to the eye, the dog must wear a tag that states that he is microchipped so that whoever picks him up will know to have him scanned. He of course also should have a tag with contact information in case his chip cannot be read.

Though less popular than microchipping, tattooing is another permanent method of ID for dogs. Most vets perform this service, and there are also clinics that perform dog tattooing. This is also an affordable procedure and one that will not cause much discomfort for the dog. It is best to put the tattoo in a visible area, such as inside the ear flap, to deter theft. It is sad to say that there are cases of dogs' being stolen and sold to research laboratories, but such laboratories will not accept tattooed dogs.

To ensure that the tattoo is effective in aiding your dog's return to you, the tattoo number must be registered with a national organization. That way, when someone finds a tattooed dog, a phone call to the registry will quickly match the dog with his owner.

BOARDING

Today there are many options for dog owners who need someone to care for their dogs in certain circumstances. While many think of boarding their dogs as something to do when away on vacation, many others use the services of doggie "daycare" facilities, dropping their dogs off to spend the day while they are at work. Many of these facilities offer both long-term and daily care. Many go beyond just boarding and cater to all sorts of needs, with on-site grooming, veterinary care, training classes and even "web-cams" where owners can log onto the Internet

You should locate a nearby boarding kennel that can safely and comfortably house your dog when you are on vacation or otherwise unable to be home with your pet.

and check out what their dogs are up to. Most dogs enjoy the activity and time spent with other dogs.

Before you need to use such a service, check out the ones in your area. Make visits to see the facilities, meet the staff, discuss fees and available services and see whether this is a place where you think your dog will be happy. It is best to do your research in advance so that you're not stuck at the last minute, forced into making a rushed decision without knowing if the kennel that you've chosen meets your standards. You also can check with your vet's office to see whether they offer boarding for their clients or can recommend a good kennel in the area.

The kennel will need to see proof of your dog's health records and vaccinations so as not to spread illness from dog to dog. Your dog also will need proper ID. Owners usually experience some separation anxiety the first time they have to leave their dog in someone else's care, so it's reassuring to know that the kennel you choose is run by experienced, caring, true dog people.

CAR CAUTION

You may like to bring your canine companion along on the daily errands, but if you will be running in and out from place to place and can't bring him indoors with you, leave him at home. Your dog should never be left alone in the car, not even for a minute—*never!* A car can heat up very quickly in even mildly warm weather, and even a cracked-open window will not help. In fact, leaving the window cracked will be dangerous if the dog becomes uncomfortable and tries to escape. When in doubt, leave your dog home, where you know he will be safe.

TRAINING YOUR

FLAT-COATED RETRIEVER

BASIC TRAINING PRINCIPLES: PUPPY VS. ADULT

There's a big difference between training an adult dog and training a young puppy. With a young puppy, everything is new! At eight to ten weeks of age, he will be experiencing many things, and he has nothing with which to compare these experiences. Up to this point, he has been with his dam and littermates, not one-on-one with people except in his interactions with his breeder and visitors to the litter.

"SCHOOL" MODE

When is your puppy ready for a lesson? Maybe not always when you are. Attempting training with treats just before his mealtime is asking for disaster. Notice what times of day he performs best and make that Fido's school time.

When you first bring your puppy home, he is eager to please you. This means that he accepts doing things your way. During the next couple of

Your Flat-Coat is a natural retriever. He will bring anything he can find to have you throw it so he can retrieve it again! You can incorporate retrieving games into teaching the pup to come to you.

months, he will absorb the basis of everything he needs to know for the rest of his life. This early age is even referred to as the "sponge" stage. After that, it's up to you to reinforce good manners on an ongoing basis by building on the foundation that you've established. Once your puppy is reliable in basic commands and behavior and has reached the appropriate age, you may gradually introduce him to some of the interesting sports, games and activities available to pet owners and their dogs.

Raising your puppy is a family affair. Each member of the family must know what rules to set forth for the puppy and how to use the same one-word commands to mean exactly the same thing every time. Even if yours is a large family, one person will soon be considered by the pup to be the leader, the Alpha person in his pack, the "boss" who must be obeyed. Often that highly regarded person turns out to be the one who feeds the puppy. Food ranks very high on the puppy's list of important things! That's why your puppy is rewarded with small treats along with verbal praise when he responds to you correctly. As the puppy learns to do what you want him to do, the food rewards are gradually eliminated and only the praise remains. If you were to keep up with the food treats, you could have two problems on your hands—an obese dog and a beggar.

Training begins the minute your Flat-Coated Retriever puppy steps through the doorway of your home, so don't make the mistake of putting the puppy on the floor and telling him by your actions to "Go for it! Run wild!" Even if this is your first puppy, you must act as if you know what you're doing: be the boss. An uncertain pup may be terrified to move, while a bold one will be ready to take you at your word and start plotting to destroy the house! Before you collected your puppy, you decided where his own special place would be, and that's where to put him when you first arrive

LEADER OF THE PACK

Canines are pack animals. They live according to pack rules, and every pack has only one leader. Guess what? That's you! To establish your position of authority, lay down the rules and be fair and good-natured in all your dealings with your dog. He will consider young children as his littermates, but the one who trains him, who feeds him, who grooms him, who expects him to come into line, that's his leader. And he who leads must be obeyed.

Flat-Coats love to please their masters and can be trained successfully for many areas of competition once they've learned the basics.

home. Give him a house tour after he has investigated his area and had a nap and a bathroom "pit stop."

It's worth mentioning here that if you've adopted an adult dog that is completely trained to your liking, lucky you! You're off the hook! However, if that dog spent his life up to this point in a kennel, or even in a good home but without any real training, be prepared to tackle the job ahead. A dog three years of age or older with no previous training cannot be blamed for not knowing what he was never taught. While the dog is trying to understand and learn your rules, at the same time he has to unlearn many of his previously self-taught habits and general view of the world.

Working with a professional trainer will speed up your progress with an adopted adult dog. You'll need patience, too. Some new rules may be close to impossible for the dog to accept. After all, he's been successful so far by doing everything his way! (Patience again.) He may agree with your instruction for a few days and then slip back into his old ways, so you must be just as consistent and understanding in your teaching as you would be with a puppy. (More patience needed yet again!) Your dog has to learn to pay attention to your voice, your family, the daily routine, new smells, new sounds and, in some cases, even a new climate.

One of the most important things to find out about a newly adopted adult dog is his reaction

I WILL FOLLOW YOU

Obedience isn't just a classroom activity. In your home you have many great opportunities to teach your dog polite manners. Allowing your pet on the bed or furniture elevates him to your level, which is not a good idea (the word is "Off!"). Use the "umbilical cord" method, keeping your dog on lead so he has to go with you wherever you go. You sit, he sits. You walk, he heels. You stop, he sit/stays. Everywhere you go, he's with you, but you go first!

SMILE WHEN YOU ORDER ME AROUND!

While trainers recommend practicing with your dog every day, it's perfectly acceptable to take a "mental health day" off. It's better not to train the dog on days when you're in a sour mood. Your bad attitude or lack of interest will be sensed by your dog, and he will respond accordingly. Studies show that dogs are well tuned in to their humans' emotions. Be conscious of how you use your voice when talking to your dog. Raising your voice or shouting will only erode your dog's trust in you as his trainer and master.

to children (yours and others), strangers and your friends, and how he acts upon meeting other dogs. If he was not socialized with dogs as a puppy, this could be a major problem. This does not mean that he's a "bad" dog, a vicious dog or an aggressive dog; rather, it means that he has no idea how to read another dog's body language. There's no way for him to tell whether the other dog is a friend or foe. Survival instinct takes over, telling him to attack first and ask questions later. This definitely calls for professional help and, even then, may not be a behavior that can be corrected 100% reliably (or even at all). If you have a puppy, this is why it is so very important to introduce your young puppy properly to other puppies and "dog-friendly" adult dogs.

HOUSE-TRAINING YOUR FLAT-COATED RETRIEVER

Dogs are tactility-oriented when it comes to house-training. In other words, they respond to the surface on which they are given approval to eliminate. The choice is yours (the dog's version is in parentheses): The lawn (including the neighbors' lawns)? A bare patch of earth under a tree (where people like to sit and relax in the summertime)? Concrete steps or patio (all sidewalks, garages and basement floors)? The curbside (watch out for cars)? A small area

Hand signals are often used along with verbal commands to teach and reinforce exercises.

EXTRA! EXTRA!

The headlines read: "Puppy Piddles Here!" Breeders commonly use newspapers to line their whelping pens, so puppies learn to associate newspapers with relieving themselves. Do not use newspapers to line your pup's crate, as this will signal to your puppy that it is OK to urinate in his crate. If you choose to paper-train your puppy, you will layer newspapers on a section of the floor near the door he uses to go outside. You should encourage the puppy to use the papers to relieve himself, and bring him there whenever you see him getting ready to go. Little by little, you will reduce the size of the newspaper-covered area so that the puppy will learn to relieve himself "on the other side of the door."

of crushed stone in a corner of the yard (mine!)? The latter is the best choice if you can manage it, because it will remain strictly for the dog's use and is easy to keep clean.

You can start out with paper-training indoors and switch over to an outdoor surface as the puppy matures and gains control over his need to eliminate. For the nay-sayers, don't worry—this won't mean that the dog will soil on every piece of newspaper lying around the house. You are training him to go outside, remember? Starting out by paper-training often is the only choice for a city dog.

When Your Puppy's "Got to Go"

Your puppy's need to relieve himself is seemingly non-stop, but signs of improvement will be seen each week. From 8 to 10 weeks old, the puppy will have to be taken outside every time he wakes up, about 10–15 minutes after every meal and after every period of play—all day long, from first thing in the morning until his bedtime! That's a total of ten or more trips per day to teach the puppy where it's okay to relieve himself. With that schedule in mind, you can see that house-

Make sure your puppy is taken to the same area each time he needs relief.

Canine Development Schedule

It is important to understand how and at what age a puppy develops into adulthood. If you are a puppy owner, consult the following Canine Development Schedule to determine the stage of development your puppy is currently experiencing. This knowledge will help you as you work with the puppy in the weeks and months ahead.

Period	Age	Characteristics
First to Third	Birth to Seven Weeks	Puppy needs food, sleep and warmth and responds to simple and gentle touching. Needs mother for security and disciplining. Needs littermates for learning and interacting with other dogs. Pup learns to function within a pack and learns pack order of dominance. Begin socializing pup with adults and children for short periods. Pup begins to become aware of his environment.
Fourth	Eight to Twelve Weeks	Brain is fully developed. Pup needs socializing with outside world. Remove from mother and littermates. Needs to change from canine pack to human pack. Human dominance necessary. Fear period occurs between 8 and 10 weeks. Avoid fright and pain.
Fifth	Thirteen to Sixteen Weeks	Training and formal obedience should begin. Less association with other dogs, more with people, places, situations. Period will pass easily if you remember this is pup's change-to-adolescence time. Be firm and fair. Flight instinct prominent. Permissiveness and over-disciplining can do permanent damage. Praise for good behavior.
Juvenile	Four to Eight Months	Another fear period about 7 to 8 months of age. It passes quickly, but be cautious of fright and pain. Sexual maturity reached. Dominant traits established. Dog should understand sit, down, come and stay by now.

Note: These are approximate time frames. Allow for individual differences in puppies.

DAILY SCHEDULE

How many relief trips does your puppy need per day? A puppy up to the age of 14 weeks will need to go outside about 8 to 12 times per day! You will have to take the pup out any time he starts sniffing around the floor or turning in small circles, as well as after naps, meals, games and lessons or whenever he's released from his crate. Once the puppy is 14 to 22 weeks of age, he will require only 6 to 8 relief trips. At the ages of 22 to 32 weeks, the puppy will require about 5 to 7 trips. Adult dogs typically require 4 relief trips per day, in the morning, afternoon, evening and late at night.

training a young puppy is not a part-time job. It requires someone to be home all day.

If that seems overwhelming or impossible, do a little planning. For example, plan to pick up your puppy at the start of a vacation period. If you can't get home in the middle of the day, plan to hire a dog-sitter or ask a neighbor to come over to take the pup outside, feed him his lunch and then take him out again about ten or so minutes after he's eaten. Also make arrangements with that or another person to be your "emergency" contact if you have to stay late on the job. Remind yourself—repeatedly—that this hectic schedule improves as the puppy gets older.

HOME WITHIN A HOME

Your Flat-Coated Retriever puppy needs to be confined to one secure, puppy-proof area when no one is able to watch his every move. Generally the kitchen is the place of choice because the floor is washable. Likewise, it's a busy family area that will accustom the pup to a variety of noises, everything from pots and pans to the telephone, blender and dishwasher. He will also be enchanted by the smell of your cooking (and will never be critical when you burn something). An exercise pen (also called an "ex-pen," a puppy version of a playpen) within the room of choice is an excellent means of confinement for a young pup. He can see out and has a certain amount of space in which to run about, but he is safe from dangerous things like

SOMEBODY TO BLAME

House-training a puppy can be frustrating for the puppy and the owner alike. The puppy does not instinctively understand the difference between defecating on the pavement outside and on the ceramic tile in the kitchen. He is confused and frightened by his human's exuberant reactions to his natural urges. The owner, arguably the more intelligent of the duo, is also frustrated that he cannot convince his puppy to obey his commands and instructions.

In frustration, the owner may struggle with the temptation to discipline the puppy, scold him or even strike him on the rear end. These types of corrections are unsuitable and unnecessary, and will defeat your purpose in gaining your puppy's trust and respect. Don't blame your nine-week-old puppy. Blame yourself for not being 100% consistent in the puppy's lessons and routine. The lesson here is simple: try harder and your puppy will succeed.

electrical cords, heating units, trash baskets or open kitchen-supply cabinets. Place the pen where the puppy will not get a blast of heat or air conditioning.

In the pen, you can put a few toys, his bed (which can be his crate if the dimensions of pen and crate are compatible) and a few layers of newspaper in one small corner, just in case. A water bowl can be hung at a convenient height on the side of the ex-pen so it won't become a splashing pool for an innovative puppy. His food dish can go on the floor, near but not under the water bowl.

Crates are something that pet owners are at last getting used to for their dogs. Wild or domestic canines have always preferred to sleep in den-like safe spots, and that is exactly what the crate provides. How often have you seen adult dogs that choose to sleep under a table or chair even though they have full run of the house? It's the den connection.

In your "happy" voice, use the word "Crate" every time you put the pup into his den. If he's new to a crate, toss in a small biscuit for him to chase the first

An "ex-pen" is easy to fold up and bring with you to provide your Flat-Coat with an area of safe confinement wherever you go.

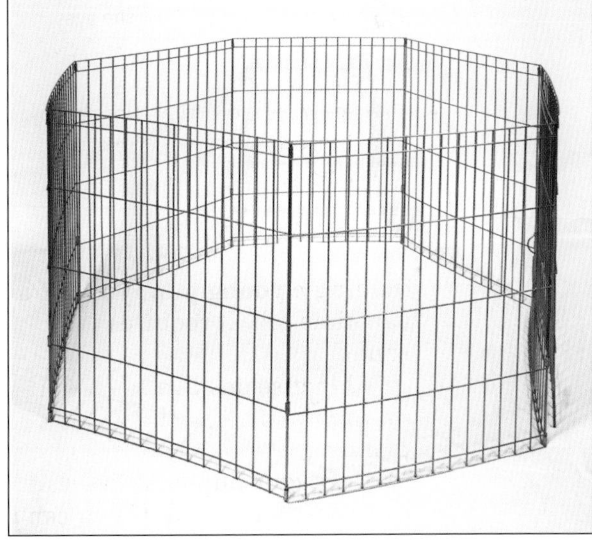

Flat-Coats are generally attentive dogs that thrive on pleasing their masters.

few times. At night, after he's been outside, he should sleep in his crate. The crate may be kept in his designated area at night or, if you want to be sure to hear those wake-up yips in the morning, put the crate in a corner of your bedroom. However, don't make any response whatsoever to whining or crying. If he's completely ignored, he'll settle down and get to sleep.

Good bedding for a young puppy is an old folded bath towel or an old blanket, something that is easily washable and disposable if necessary ("accidents" will happen!). Never put newspaper in the puppy's crate. Also, those old ideas about adding a clock to replace his mother's heartbeat, or a hot-water bottle to replace her warmth, are just that—old ideas. The clock could drive the puppy nuts, and the hot-water bottle could end up as a very soggy waterbed! An extremely good breeder would have introduced your puppy to the crate by letting two pups sleep together for a couple of nights, followed by several nights alone. How thankful you will be if you found that breeder!

Safe toys in the pup's crate or area will keep him occupied, but monitor their condition closely. Discard any toys that show signs of being chewed to bits. Squeaky

POTTY COMMAND

Most dogs love to please their masters; there are no bounds to what dogs will do to make their owners happy. The potty command is a good example of this theory. If toileting on command makes the master happy, then more power to him. Puppies will obligingly piddle if it really makes their keepers smile. Some owners can be creative about which word they will use to command their dogs to relieve themselves. Some popular choices are "Potty," "Tinkle," "Piddle," "Let's go," "Hurry up" and "Toilet." Give the command every time your puppy goes into position and the puppy will begin to associate his business with the command.

OUR CANINE KIDS

"Everything I learned about parenting, I learned from my dog." How often adults recognize that their parenting skills are mere extensions of the education they acquired while caring for their dogs. Many owners refer to their dogs as their "kids" and treat their canine companions like real members of the family. Surveys indicate that a majority of dog owners talk to their dogs regularly, celebrate their dogs' birthdays and purchase Christmas gifts for their dogs. Another survey shows that dog owners take their dogs to the veterinarian more frequently than they visit their own physicians.

parts, bits of stuffing or plastic or any other small pieces can cause intestinal blockage or possibly choking if swallowed.

Progressing with Potty-Training

After you've taken your puppy out and he has relieved himself in the area you've selected, he can have some free time with the family as long as there is someone responsible for watching him. That doesn't mean just someone in the same room who is watching TV or busy on the computer, but one person who is doing nothing other than keeping an eye on the pup, playing with him on the floor and helping him understand his position in the pack.

This first taste of freedom will let you begin to set the house rules. If you don't want the dog on the furniture, now is the time to prevent his first attempts to jump up onto the couch. The word to use in this case is "Off," not "Down." "Down" is the word you will use to teach the down position, which is something entirely different.

Most corrections at this stage come in the form of simply distracting the puppy. Instead of telling him "No" for "Don't chew the carpet," distract the chomping puppy with a toy and he'll forget about the carpet.

As you are playing with the pup, do not forget to watch him closely and pay attention to his body language. Whenever you

You want your Flat-Coat to accept his crate as his private den, his very own special place.

see him begin to circle or sniff, take the puppy outside to relieve himself. If you are paper-training, put him back into his confined area on the newspapers. In either case, praise him as he eliminates while he actually is *in the act* of relieving himself. Three seconds after he has finished is too late! You'll be praising him for running toward you, or picking up a toy or whatever he may be doing at that moment, and that's not what you want to be praising him for. Timing is a vital tool in all dog training. Use it.

Remove soiled newspapers immediately and replace them with clean ones. You may want to take a small piece of soiled paper and place it in the middle of the new clean papers, as the scent will attract him to that spot when it's time to go again. That scent attraction is why it's so important to clean up any messes made in the house by using a product specially made to eliminate the odor of dog urine and droppings. Regular household cleansers won't do the trick. Pet shops sell the best pet-odor deodorizers. Invest in the largest container!

Scent attraction eventually will lead your pup to his chosen spot outdoors; this is the basis of outdoor training. When you take your puppy outside to relieve himself, use a one-word command such as "Outside" or "Go-potty" (that's one word to the puppy!) as you pick him up and attach his leash. Then put him down in his area. If for any reason you can't carry him, snap the leash on quickly and lead him to his spot. Now comes the hard part—hard for you, that is. Just stand there until he urinates and defecates. Move him a few feet in one direction or another if he's just sitting there looking at you, but

LEASH TRAINING

House-training and leash training go hand in hand, literally. When taking your puppy outside to do his business, lead him there on his leash. Unless an emergency potty run is called for, do not whisk the puppy up into your arms and take him outside. If you have a fenced yard, you have the advantage of letting the puppy loose to go out, but it's better to put the dog on the leash and take him to his designated place in the yard until he is reliably house-trained. Taking the puppy for a walk is the best way to house-train a dog. The dog will associate the walk with his time to relieve himself, and the exercise of walking stimulates the dog's bowels and bladder. Dogs that are not trained to relieve themselves on a walk may hold it until they get back home, which of course defeats half the purpose of the walk.

remember that this is neither playtime nor time for a walk. This is strictly a business trip! Then, as he circles and squats (remember your timing!), give him a quiet "Good dog" as praise. If you start to jump for joy, ecstatic over his performance, he'll do one of two things: either he will stop midstream, as it were, or he'll do it again for you—in the house—and expect you to be just as delighted!

Give him five minutes or so and, if he doesn't go in that time, take him back indoors to his confined area and try again in another ten minutes, or immediately if you see him sniffing and circling. By careful observation, you'll soon work out a successful schedule.

Accidents, by the way, are just that—accidents. Clean them up quickly and thoroughly, without comment, after the puppy has been taken outside to finish his business and then put back into his area or crate. If you witness an accident in progress, say "No!" in a stern voice and get the pup outdoors immediately. No punishment is needed. You and your puppy are just learning each other's language, and sometimes it's easy to miss a puppy's message. Chalk it up to experience and watch more closely from now on.

TIDY BOY

Clean by nature, dogs do not like to soil their dens, which in effect are their crates or sleeping quarters. Unless not feeling well, dogs will not defecate or urinate in their crates. Crate training capitalizes on the dog's natural desire to keep his den clean. Be conscientious about giving the puppy as many opportunities to relieve himself outdoors as possible. Reward the puppy for correct behavior. Praise him and pat him whenever he "goes" in the correct location. Even the tidiest of puppies can have potty accidents, so be patient and dedicate more energy to helping your puppy achieve a clean lifestyle.

KEEPING THE PACK ORDERLY

Discipline is a form of training that brings order to life. For example, military discipline is what allows the soldiers in an army to work as one. Discipline is a form of teaching and, in dogs, is the basis of how the successful pack operates. Each member knows his place in the pack and all respect the leader, or Alpha dog. It is essential for your puppy that you establish this type of relationship, with you as the Alpha, or leader. It is a form of social coexistence that all canines recognize and accept. Discipline, therefore, is never to be confused with punishment. When you teach your puppy how you want him to behave, and he behaves properly and you praise him for it, you are disciplining him with a form of positive reinforcement.

For a dog, rewards come in the form of praise, a smile, a cheerful tone of voice, a few friendly pats or a rub of the ears. Rewards are also small food treats. Obviously, that does not mean bits of regular dog food. Instead, treats are very small bits of special things like cheese or pieces of soft dog treats. The idea is to reward the dog with something very small that he can taste and swallow, providing instant positive reinforcement. If he has to take time to chew the treat, by the time he is finished he will have forgotten what he did to earn it!

Your puppy should never be physically punished. The

TIME TO PLAY!

Playtime can happen both indoors and out. A young puppy is growing so rapidly that he needs sleep more than he needs a lot of physical exercise. Puppies get sufficient exercise on their own just through normal puppy activity. Monitor play with young children so you can remove the puppy when he's had enough, or calm the kids if they get too rowdy. Almost all puppies love to chase after a toy you've thrown, and you can turn your games into educational activities. Every time your puppy brings the toy back to you, say "Give it" (or "Drop it") followed by "Good dog" and throwing it again. If he's reluctant to give it to you, offer a small treat so that he drops the toy as he takes the treat. He will soon get the idea.

In competitive pursuits like obedience and agility, the dog's performance is tested as well as the teamwork between dog and owner.

A pup will always come to you when a tasty morsel is at stake!

displeasure shown on your face and in your voice is sufficient to signal to the pup that he has done something wrong. The Flat-Coat does not respond well to harsh corrections. He wants to please everyone higher up on the social ladder, especially his leader, so a scowl and a disapproving tone of voice will take care of the error. Growling out the word "Shame!" when the pup is caught in the act of doing something wrong is better than the repetitive "No." Some dogs hear "No" so often that they begin to think it's their name! By the way, do not use the dog's name when you're correcting him. His name is reserved to get his attention for something pleasant about to take place.

There are punishments that have nothing to do with you. For example, your dog may think that chasing cats is one reason for his existence. You can try to stop it as much as you like but

BASIC PRINCIPLES OF DOG TRAINING

1. Start training early. A young puppy is ready, willing and able.
2. Timing is your all-important tool. Praise at the exact time that the dog responds correctly. Pay close attention.
3. Patience is almost as important as timing!
4. Repeat! The same word has to mean the same thing every time.
5. In the beginning, praise all correct behavior verbally, along with treats and petting.

Follow the leader! Young puppies generally will stay close by—until curiosity takes over!

without success, because it's such fun for the dog. But one good hissing, spitting swipe of a cat's claws across the dog's nose will put an end to the game forever. Intervene only when your dog's eyeball is seriously at risk. Cat scratches can cause permanent damage to an innocent but annoying puppy.

PUPPY KINDERGARTEN

Collar and Leash

Before you begin your Flat-Coated Retriever puppy's education, he must be used to his collar and leash. Choose a collar for your puppy that is secure, but not heavy or bulky. He won't enjoy training if he's uncomfortable. A flat buckle collar is fine for everyday wear and for initial puppy training. For older puppies and adult dogs, there are several types of training collars such as the martingale, which is a double loop that tightens slightly around the neck, or the head collar, which is similar to a horse's halter. Both of these options are better for the Flat-Coat than the choke collar; always ask the advice of your breeder or a trainer before choosing a training collar for your Flat-Coat.

A lightweight 6-foot woven cotton or nylon training leash is preferred by most trainers because it is easy to fold up in your hand and comfortable to hold because there is a certain amount of give to it. There are lessons where the dog will start

TIPS FOR TRAINING AND SAFETY

1. Whether on- or off-leash, practice only in a fenced area.
2. Remove the training collar when the training session is over.
3. Don't try to break up a dog-fight.
4. "Come," "Leave it" and "Wait" are safety commands.
5. The dog belongs in a crate or behind a barrier when riding in the car.
6. Don't ignore the dog's first sign of aggression. Aggression only gets worse, so take it seriously.
7. Keep the faces of children and dogs separated.
8. Pay attention to what the dog is chewing.
9. Keep the vet's number near your phone.
10. "Okay" is a useful release command.

The first step in training is to get the dog's attention and keep it. These two Flat-Coats eagerly await the next command from their master.

off 6 feet away from you at the end of the leash. The leash used to take the puppy outside to relieve himself is shorter because you don't want him to roam away from his area. The shorter leash will also be the one to use initially when you walk the pup.

If you've been wise enough to enroll in a Puppy Kindergarten training class, suggestions will be made as to the best collar and leash for your young puppy. I say "wise" because your puppy will be in a class with puppies in his age range (up to five months old) of all breeds and sizes. It's the perfect way for him to learn the right way (and the wrong way) to interact with other dogs as well as their people. You cannot teach your puppy how to interpret another dog's sign language. For a first-time puppy owner, these socialization classes are invaluable. For experienced dog owners, they are a real boon to further training.

Attention

You've been using the dog's name since the minute you collected him from the breeder, so you should be able to get his attention by saying his name—with a big smile and in an excited tone of voice. His response will be the puppy equivalent of "Here I am! What are we going to do?" Your immediate response (if you haven't guessed by now) is "Good dog." Rewarding him at the moment he pays attention to you teaches him the proper way to respond when he hears his name.

EXERCISES FOR A BASIC CANINE EDUCATION

The Sit Exercise

There are several ways to teach the puppy to sit. The first one is to catch him whenever he is about to sit and, as his backside nears the floor, say "Sit, good dog!" That's positive reinforce-

A SIMPLE "SIT"

When you command your dog to sit, use the word "Sit." Do not say "Sit down," as your dog will not know whether you mean "Sit" or "Down," or maybe you mean both. Be clear in your instructions to your dog; use one-word commands and always be consistent.

READY, SIT, GO!

On your marks, get set: train! Most professional trainers agree that the sit command is the place to start your dog's formal education. Sitting is a natural posture for most dogs, and they respond to the sit exercise willingly and readily. For every lesson, begin with the sit command so that you start out with a successful exercise; likewise, you should practice the sit command at the end of every lesson as well, because you always want to end on a high note.

ment and, if your timing is sharp, he will learn that what he's doing at that second is connected to your saying "Sit" and that you think he's clever for doing it!

Another method is to start with the puppy on his leash in front of you. Show him a treat in the palm of your right hand. Bring your hand up under his nose and, almost in slow motion, move your hand up and back so his nose goes up in the air and his head tilts back as he follows the treat in your hand. At that point, he will have to either sit or fall over, so as his back legs buckle under, say "Sit, good dog," and then give him the treat and lots of praise. You may have to begin with your hand lightly running up his chest, actually lifting his chin up until he sits. Some (usually older) dogs require gentle pressure on their hindquarters with the left hand, in which case the dog should be on your left side. Puppies generally do not appreciate this physical dominance.

After a few times, you should be able to show the dog a treat in the open palm of your hand, raise your hand waist-high as you say "Sit" and have him sit. You thereby will have taught him two things at the same time. Both the verbal command and the motion of the hand are signals for the sit. Your puppy is watching you almost more than he is listening to you, so what you do is just as important as what you say.

Don't save any of these drills only for training sessions. Use them as much as possible at odd times during a normal day. The dog should always sit before being given his food dish. He should sit to let you go through a doorway first, when the doorbell rings or when you stop to speak to someone on the street.

The Down Exercise

Before beginning to teach the down command, you must consider how the dog feels about this exercise. To him, "Down" is a submissive position. Being flat on the floor with you standing over him is not his idea of fun. It's up to you to let him know that, while it may not be fun, the reward of your approval is worth his effort.

Start with the puppy on your left side in a sit position. Hold the leash right above his collar in your left hand. Have an extra-special treat, such as a small piece of cooked chicken or hot dog, in your right hand. Place it at the end of the pup's nose and steadily move your hand down and forward along the ground. Hold the leash to prevent a sudden lunge for the food. As the puppy goes into the down position, say "Down" very gently.

The difficulty with this exercise is twofold: it's both the submissive aspect and the fact that most people say the word "Down" as if they were drill sergeants in charge of recruits! So issue the command sweetly, give him the treat and have the pup maintain the down position for several seconds. If he tries to get up immediately, place your hands on his shoulders and press down gently, giving him a very quiet "Good dog." As you progress with this lesson, increase the "down time" until he will hold it until you say "Okay" (his cue for release). Practice this one in the house at various times throughout the day.

By increasing the length of time during which the dog must maintain the down position, you'll find many uses for it. For example, he can lie at your feet in the vet's office or anywhere that both of you have to wait, when you are on the phone, while the family is eating and so forth. If you progress to training for competitive obedience, he'll already be all set for the exercise called the "long down."

DOWN

"Down" is a harsh-sounding word and a submissive posture in dog body language, thus presenting two obstacles in teaching the down command. When the dog is about to flop down on his own, tell him "Good down." Pups that are not good about being handled learn better by having food lowered in front of them. A dog that trusts you can be gently guided into position. When you give the command "Down," be sure to say it sweetly!

The Stay Exercise

You can teach your Flat-Coated Retriever to stay in the sit, down and stand positions. To teach the sit/stay, have the dog sit on your left side. Hold the leash at waist level in your left hand and let the dog know that you have a treat in your closed right hand. Step forward on your right foot as you say "Stay." Immediately turn and stand directly in front of the dog, keeping your right hand up high so he'll keep his eye on the treat hand and maintain the sit position for a count of five. Return to your original position and offer the reward.

Formal retrieving training can begin once your Flat-Coat has mastered the basics. It will be fun and come naturally to him—after all, "retriever" is his last name!

OKAY!

This is the signal that tells your dog that he can quit whatever he was doing. Use "Okay" to end a session on a correct response to a command. (Never end on an incorrect response.) Lots of praise follows. People use "Okay" a lot and it has other uses for dogs, too. Your dog is barking. You say, "Okay! Come!" "Okay" signals him to stop the barking activity and "Come" allows him to come to you for a "Good dog."

Increase the length of the sit/stay each time until the dog can hold it for at least 30 seconds without moving. After about a week of success, move out on your right foot and take two steps before turning to face the dog. Give the "Stay" hand signal (left palm back toward the dog's head) as you leave. He gets the treat when you return and he holds the sit/stay. Increase the distance that you walk away from him before turning until you reach the length of your training leash. But don't rush it! Go back to the beginning if he moves before he should. No matter what the lesson, never be upset by having to back up for a few days. The repetition and practice are what will make your dog reliable in these commands. It won't do any good to move on to something more difficult if the command is not mastered at the easier levels. Above all, even if you do get frustrated, never let your puppy know! Always keep a positive, upbeat attitude during training, which will transmit to

RIGHT CLICK ON YOUR DOG

With three clicks, the dolphin jumps through the hoop. Wouldn't it be nice to have a dog who could obey wordless commands that easily? Clicker training actually was developed by dolphin trainers and today is used on dogs with great success. You can buy a clicker at a pet shop or pet-supply outlet, and then you'll be off and clicking.

You can click your dog into learning new commands, shaping or conditioning his behavior and solving bad habits. The clicker, used in conjunction with a treat, is an extension of positive reinforcement. The dog begins to recognize your happy clicking, which becomes sufficient as a reward. The dog is conditioned to follow your hand with the clicker, just as he would follow your hand with a treat. To discourage the dog from inappropriate behavior (like jumping up or barking), you can use the clicker to set a timeframe and then click and reward the dog once he's waited the allotted time without jumping up or barking.

your dog for positive results.

The down/stay is taught in the same way once the dog is completely reliable and steady with the down command. Again, don't rush it. With the dog in the down position on your left side, step out on your right foot as you say "Stay." Return by walking around in back of the dog and into your original position. While you are training, it's okay to murmur something like "Hold on" to encourage him to stay put. When the dog will stay without moving when you are at a distance of 3 or 4 feet, begin to increase the length of time before you return. Be sure he holds the down on your return until you say "Okay." At that point, he gets his treat—just so he'll remember for next time that it's not over until it's over.

The Come Exercise

No command is more important to the safety of your Flat-Coated Retriever than "Come." It is what you should say every single time you see the puppy running toward you: "Binky, come! Good dog." During playtime, run a few feet away from the puppy and turn and tell him to "Come" as he is already running to you. You can go so far as to teach your puppy two things at once if you squat down and hold out your arms. As the pup gets close to you and you're saying "Good

The come command is one of the most important things you can teach your Flat-Coat for his safety.

dog," bring your right arm in about waist high. Now he's also learning the hand signal, an excellent device should you be on the phone when you need to get him to come to you! You'll also both be one step ahead when you enter obedience classes.

When the puppy responds to your well-timed "Come," try it with the puppy on the training leash. This time, catch him off guard, while he's sniffing a leaf or watching a bird: "Binky, come!" You may have to pause for a split second after his name to be sure you have his attention. If the puppy shows any sign of confusion, give the leash a mild jerk and take a couple of steps backward. Do not repeat the command. In this case, you

COME AND GET IT!

The come command is your dog's safety signal. Until he is 99% perfect in responding, don't use the come command if you cannot enforce it. Practice on leash with treats or squeakers, or whenever the dog is running to you. Never call him to come to you if he is to be corrected for a misdemeanor. Reward the dog with a treat and happy praise whenever he comes to you.

LET'S GO!

Many people use "Let's go" instead of "Heel" when teaching their dogs to behave on lead. It sounds like more fun! When beginning to teach the heel, whatever command you use, always step off on your left foot. That's the one next to the dog, who is on your left side, in case you've forgotten. Keep a loose leash. When the dog pulls ahead, stop, bring him back and begin again. Use treats to guide him around turns.

should say "Good come" as he reaches you.

That's the number-one rule of training. Each command word is given just once. Anything more is nagging. You'll also notice that all commands are one word only. Even when they are actually two words, you say them as one.

Never call the dog to come to you—with or without his name—if you are angry or intend to correct him for some misbehavior. When correcting the pup, you go to him. Your dog must always connect "Come" with something pleasant and with your approval; then you can rely on his response.

Puppies, like children, have notoriously short attention spans, so don't overdo it with any of the training. Keep each lesson short. Break it up with a quick run around the yard or a ball toss, repeat the lesson and quit as soon as the pup gets it right. That way, you will always end with a "Good dog."

Life isn't perfect and neither are puppies. A time will come, often around ten months of age, when he'll become "selectively deaf" or choose to "forget" his name. He may respond by wagging his tail (and even seeming to smile at you) with a look that says "Make me!" Laugh, throw his favorite toy and skip the lesson you had planned. Pups will be pups!

The Heel Exercise

The second most important command to teach, after the come, is the heel. When you are walking your growing puppy, you need to be in control. Besides, it looks terrible to be pulled and yanked down the street, and it's not much fun either. Your eight- to ten-week-old puppy will probably follow you everywhere, but that's his natural instinct, not your control over the situation. However, any time he does follow you, you can say "Heel" and be ahead of the game, as he will learn to associate this command with the action of following you before you even begin teaching him to heel.

There is a very precise, almost military, procedure for teaching your dog to heel. As

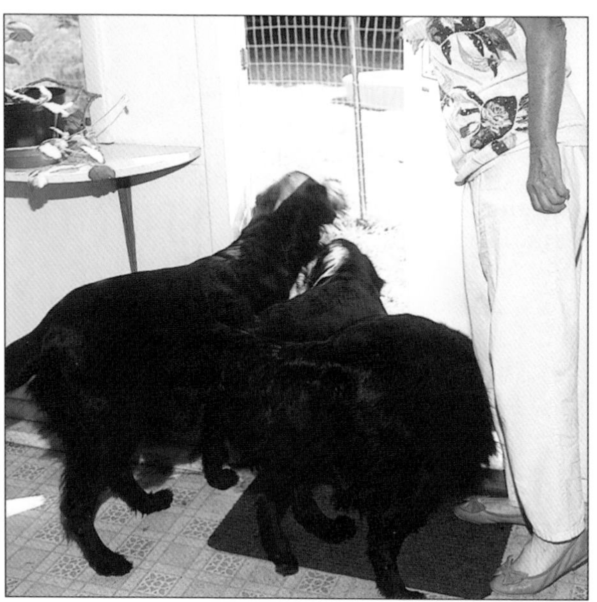

A big part of training your dog is establishing the daily routine. This Flat-Coat clan knows when it's time to go outside!

with all other obedience training, begin with the dog on your left side. He will be in a very nice sit and you will have the training leash across your chest. Hold the loop and folded leash in your right hand. Pick up the slack leash above the dog in your left hand and hold it loosely at your side. Step out on your left foot as you say "Heel." If the puppy does not move, give a gentle tug or pat your left leg to get him started. If he surges ahead of you, stop and pull him back gently until he is at your side. Tell him to sit and begin again.

Walk a few steps and stop while the puppy is correctly beside you. Tell him to sit and give mild verbal praise. (More enthusiastic praise will encourage him to think the lesson is over.) Repeat the lesson, increasing the number of steps you take only as long as the dog is heeling nicely beside you. When you end the lesson, have him hold the sit, then give him the "Okay" to let him know that this is the end of the lesson. Praise him so that he knows he did a good job.

The cure for excessive pulling (a common problem) is to stop when the dog is no more than 2 or 3 feet ahead of you. Guide him back into position and begin again. With a really determined puller, try switching to a head collar. This will automatically turn the pup's head toward you so you can bring him back easily to the heel position. Give quiet, reassuring praise every time the leash goes slack and he's staying with you.

Staying and heeling can take a lot out of a dog, so provide playtime and free-running exercise to shake off the stress when the lessons are over. You don't want him to associate training with all work and no fun.

TAPERING OFF TIDBITS

Your dog has been watching you—and the hand that treats—throughout all of his lessons, and now it's time to break the treat habit. Begin by giving him treats at the end of each lesson only. Then start to give a treat after the end of only some of the lessons. At the end of every lesson, as well as during the lessons, be consistent with the praise. Your pup now doesn't know whether he'll get a treat or not, but he should keep performing well just in case! Finally, you will stop giving treat rewards entirely. Save them for something brand-new that you want to teach him. Keep up the praise and you'll always have a "good dog."

OBEDIENCE CLASSES

The advantages of an obedience class are that your dog will have to learn amid the distractions of other people and dogs and that your mistakes will be quickly corrected by the trainer. Teaching your dog along with a qualified instructor and other handlers who may have more dog experience than you is another plus of the class environment. The instructor and other handlers can help you to find the most efficient way of teaching your dog a command or exercise. It's often easier to learn by other people's mistakes than your own. You will also learn all of the requirements for competitive obedience trials, in which you can earn titles and go on to advanced jumping and retrieving exercises, which are fun for many dogs. Obedience classes build the foundation needed for many other canine activities (in which we humans are allowed to participate, too!).

OTHER ACTIVITIES FOR LIFE

Whether a dog is trained in the structured environment of a class or alone with his owner at home, there are many activities that can bring fun and rewards to both owner and dog once they have mastered basic control. Teaching the dog to help out around the home, in

DON'T STRESS ME OUT

Your dog doesn't have to deal with paying the bills, the daily commute, PTA meetings and the like, but, believe it or not, there is a lot of stress in a dog's world. Stress can be caused by the owner's impatient demeanor and his angry or harsh corrections. If your dog cringes when you reach for his training collar, he's stressed. An older dog is sometimes stressed out when he goes to a new home. No matter what the cause, put off all training until he's over it. If he's going through a fear period—shying away from people, trembling when spoken to, avoiding eye contact or hiding under furniture—wait to resume training. Naturally you'd also postpone your lessons if the dog were sick, and the same goes for you. Show some compassion.

the yard or on the farm provides great satisfaction to both dog and owner. In addition, the dog's help makes life a little easier for his owner and raises his stature as a valued companion to his family. It helps give the dog a purpose by occupying his mind and providing an outlet for his energy.

For a retriever, nothing is as fulfilling as hunting! Whether you take your Flat-Coated Retriever into the woods for a Saturday exhibition or plan to compete with your dog in a field trial, your Flat-Coat will prove how strong his hunting instincts still are! Fortunately, the Flat-Coat can still boast his ancestral abilities, and an interested owner can get involved in many field-related activities.

Flat-Coated Retrievers are very athletic and will enjoy being trained for agility trials and obedience competition.

For an endeavor less complicated than field trials and hunting events, backpacking is an exciting and healthy activity that the dog can be taught without assistance from more than his owner. The exercise of walking and climbing is good for man and dog alike, and the bond that they develop together is priceless. Hiking is another great activity for the Flat-Coat, especially if you have woods or a park nearby.

If you are interested in participating in organized competition with your Flat-Coat, there are activities other than field events and obedience trials in which you and your dog can become involved. Agility is a sport in which dogs run through an obstacle course that includes various jumps, tunnels and other exercises to test the dogs' speed and coordination. The owners run through the course beside their dogs to give commands and to guide them through the course. Although competitive, the focus is on fun—it's fun to do, fun to watch and great exercise. You can also look into flyball and disc-catching competitions—the Flat-Coat is anxious to retrieve anything from flying discs to fallen ducks! Get your Flat-Coat involved in some activities and you will both be the healthier and happier for it.

Two well-trained Flat-Coats pose politely for a portrait.

PHYSICAL STRUCTURE OF THE FLAT-COATED RETRIEVER

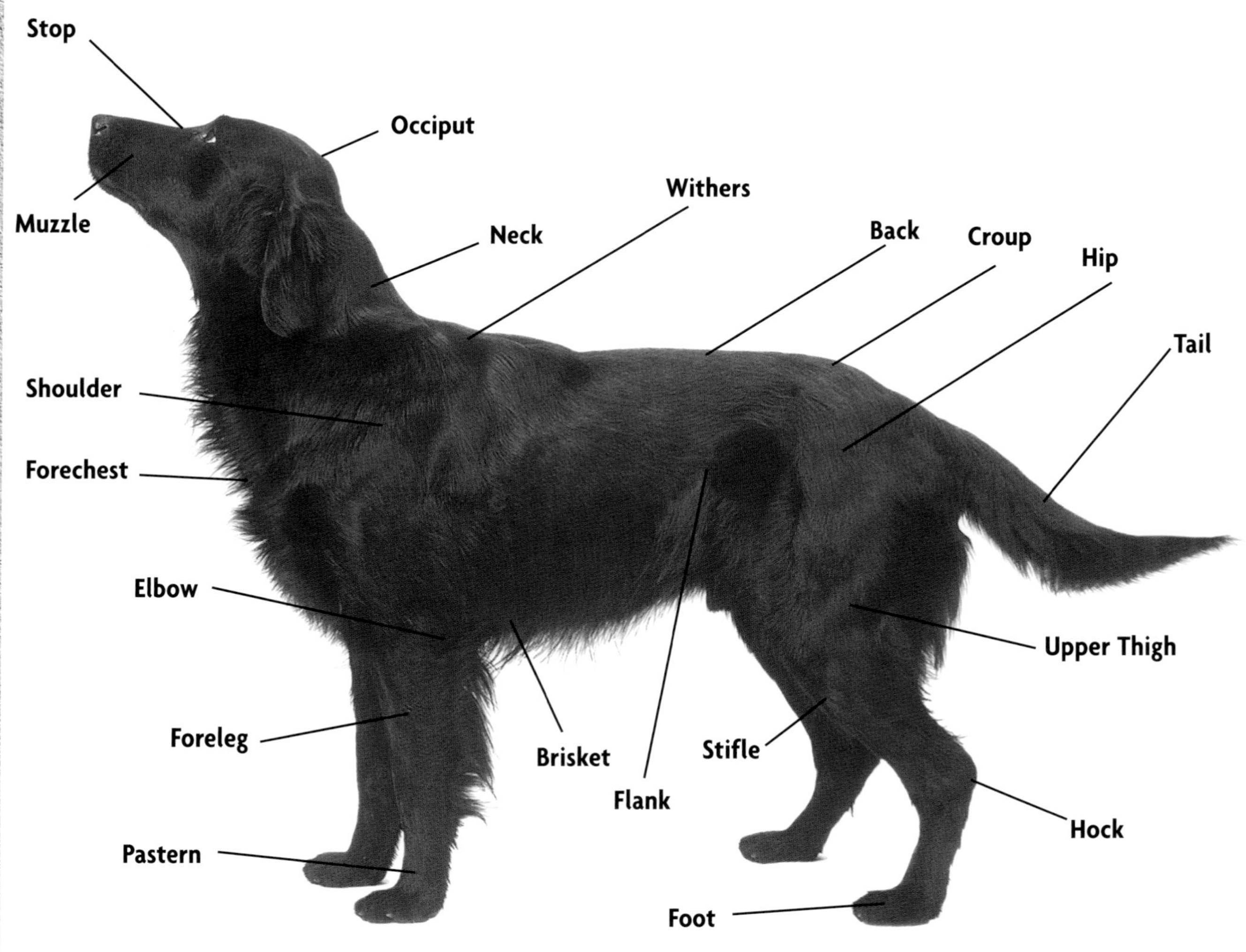

HEALTHCARE OF YOUR

FLAT-COATED RETRIEVER

BY LOWELL ACKERMAN DVM, DACVD

HEALTHCARE FOR A LIFETIME

When you own a dog, you become his healthcare advocate over his entire lifespan, as well as being the one to shoulder the financial burden of such care. Accordingly, it is worthwhile to focus on prevention rather than treatment, as you and your pet will both be happier.

Of course, the best place to have begun your program of preventive healthcare is with the initial purchase or adoption of your dog. There is no way of guaranteeing that your new furry friend is free of medical problems, but there are some things you can do to improve your odds. You certainly should have done adequate research into the Flat-Coated Retriever and have selected your puppy carefully rather than buying on impulse. Health issues aside, a large number of pet abandonment and relinquishment cases arise from a mismatch between pet needs and owner expectations. This is entirely preventable with appropriate planning and finding a good breeder.

Regarding healthcare issues specifically, it is very difficult to make blanket statements about where to acquire a problem-free pet, but, again, a reputable breeder is your best bet. In an ideal situation, you have the opportunity to see both parents, get references from other owners of the breeder's pups and see genetic-testing documentation for several generations of the litter's ancestors. At the very least, you must thoroughly investigate the Flat-Coated Retriever and the problems inherent in the breed, as well as the genetic testing available to screen for those problems. Genetic testing offers some important benefits, but testing is available for only a few disorders in a relatively small number of breeds and is not available for some of

Before you buy a dog, meet and interview the vet in your area. Take everything into consideration; discuss background, specialties, fees, emergency policies, etc.

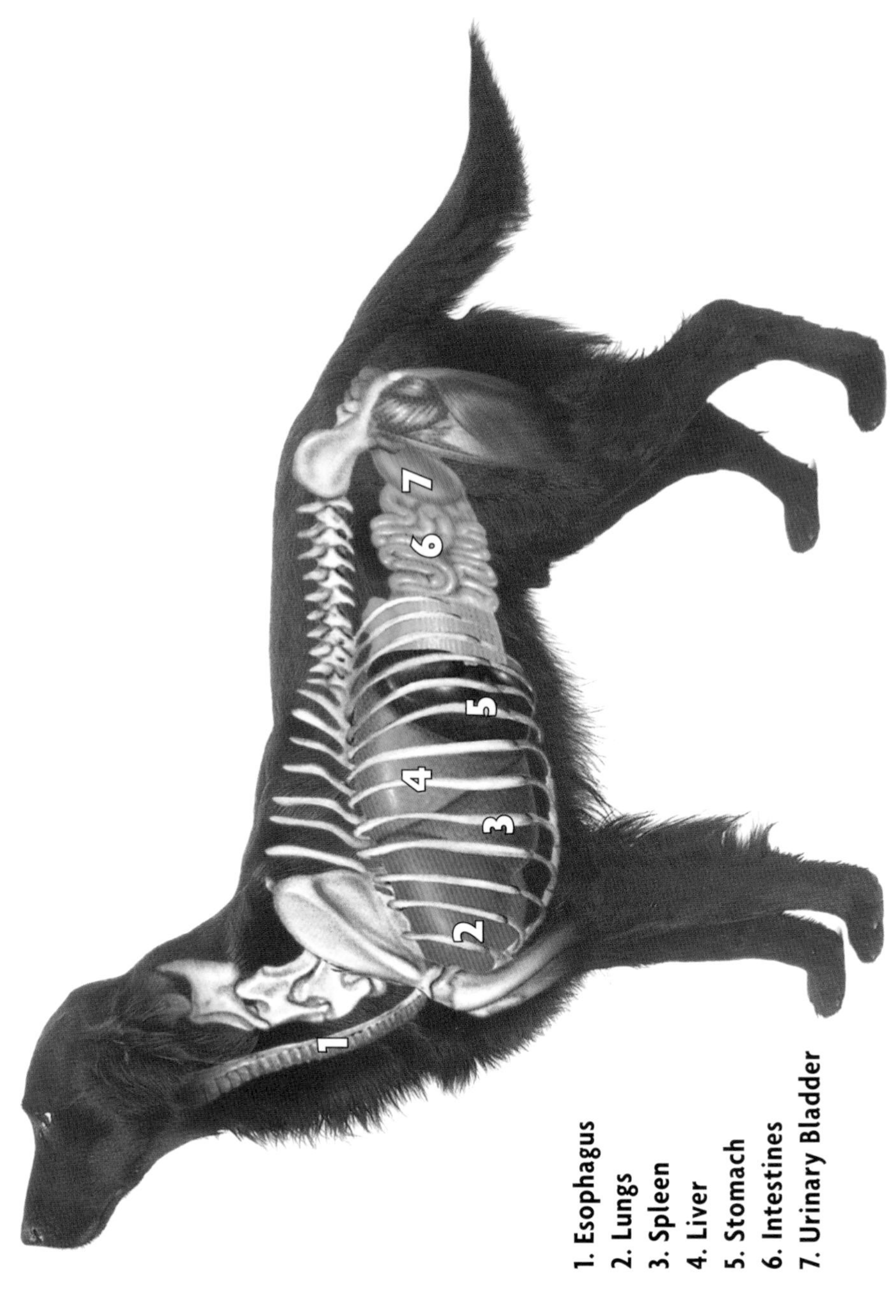

INTERNAL ORGANS OF THE FLAT-COATED RETRIEVER

the most common genetic diseases, such as hip dysplasia, cataracts, epilepsy, cardiomyopathy, etc. This area of research is indeed exciting and increasingly important, and advances will continue to be made each year. In fact, recent research has shown that there is an equivalent dog gene for 75% of known human genes, so research done in either species is likely to benefit the other.

TAKING YOUR DOG'S TEMPERATURE

It is important to know how to take your dog's temperature at times when you think he may be ill. It's not the most enjoyable task, but it can be done without too much difficulty. It's easier with a helper, preferably someone with whom the dog is friendly, so that one of you can hold the dog while the other inserts the thermometer.

Before inserting the thermometer, coat the end with petroleum jelly. Insert the thermometer slowly and gently into the dog's rectum about one inch. Wait for the reading, about two minutes. Be sure to remove the thermometer carefully and clean it thoroughly after each use.

A dog's normal body temperature is between 100.5 and 102.5 degrees F. Immediate veterinary attention is required if the dog's temperature is below 99 or above 104 degrees F.

We've also discussed that evaluating the behavioral nature of your Flat-Coated Retriever and that of his immediate family members is an important part of the selection process that cannot be underestimated or overemphasized. It is sometimes difficult to evaluate temperament in puppies because certain behavioral tendencies, such as some forms of aggression, may not be immediately evident. More dogs are euthanized each year for behavioral reasons than for all medical conditions combined, so it is critical to take temperament issues seriously. Start with a well-balanced, friendly companion and put the time and effort into proper socialization, and you will both be rewarded with a lifelong valued relationship.

Assuming that you have started off with a pup from healthy, sound stock, you then become responsible for helping your veterinarian keep your pet healthy. Some crucial things happen before you even bring your puppy home. Parasite control typically begins at two weeks of age, and vaccinations typically begin at six to eight weeks of age. A pre-pubertal evaluation is typically scheduled for about six months of age. At this time, a dental evaluation is done (since the adult teeth are now in), heartworm prevention is started and neutering or spaying is most commonly done.

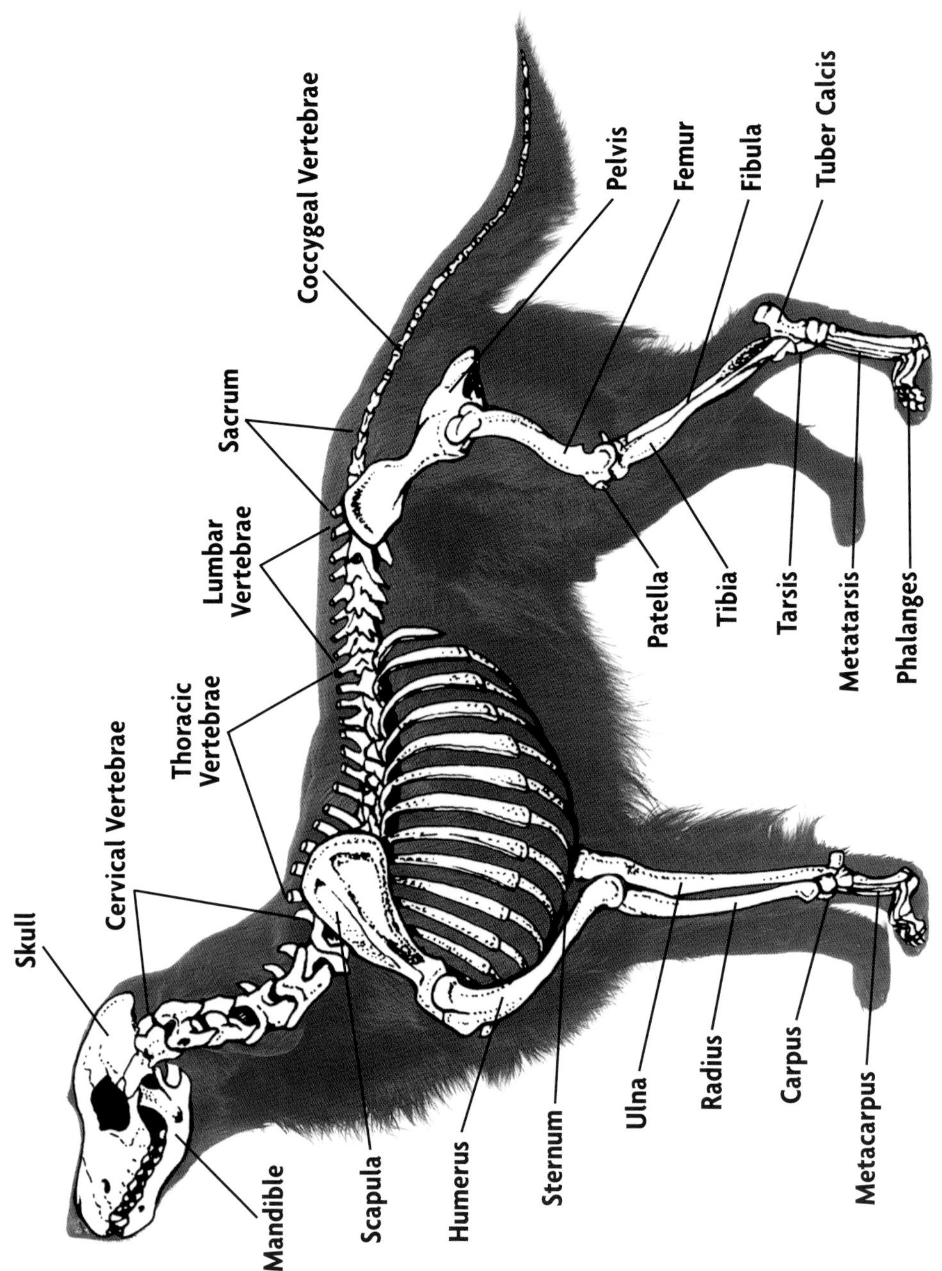

SKELETAL STRUCTURE OF THE FLAT-COATED RETRIEVER

DOGGIE DENTAL DON'TS

A veterinary dental exam is necessary if you notice one or any combination of the following in your dog:

- Broken, loose or missing teeth
- Loss of appetite (which could be due to mouth pain or illness caused by infection)
- Gum abnormalities, including redness, swelling and bleeding
- Drooling, with or without blood
- Yellowing of the teeth or gumline, indicating tartar
- Bad breath

It is critical to commence regular dental care at home if you have not already done so. It may not sound very important, but most dogs have active periodontal disease by four years of age if they don't have their teeth cleaned regularly at home, not just at their veterinary exams. Dental problems lead to more than just bad "doggie breath." Gum disease can have very serious medical consequences. If you start brushing your dog's teeth and using antiseptic rinses from a young age, your dog will be accustomed to it and will not resist. The results will be healthy dentition, which your pet will need to enjoy a long, healthy life.

Most dogs are considered adults at a year of age, although the Flat-Coat is a slow-maturing breed and isn't considered fully mature until about three or so years old. Even individual dogs within each breed have different healthcare requirements, so work with your veterinarian to determine what will be needed and what your role should be. This doctor-client relationship is important, because as vaccination guidelines change, there may not be an annual "vaccine visit" scheduled. You must make sure that you see your veterinarian at least annually, even if no vaccines are due, because this is the best opportunity to coordinate healthcare activities and to make sure

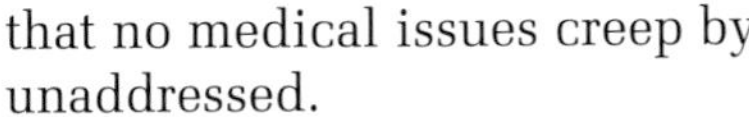

that no medical issues creep by unaddressed.

When your Flat-Coated Retriever reaches three-quarters of his anticipated lifespan, he is considered a "senior" and likely requires some special care. In general, if you've been taking great care of your canine companion throughout his formative and adult years, the transition to senior status should be a smooth one. Age is not a disease, and as long as everything is functioning as it should, there is no reason why most of late adulthood should not be rewarding for both you and your pet. This is especially true if you have tended to the details, such as regular veterinary visits, proper dental care, excellent nutrition and management of bone and joint issues.

WHAT IS "BLOAT"?

Need yet another reason to avoid tossing your dog a morsel from your plate? It is shown that dogs fed table scraps have an increased risk of developing bloat, or gastric torsion. Did you know that more occurrences of bloat occur in the warm-weather months due to the frequency of outdoor cooking and dining and dogs' receiving "samples" from the fired-up grill?

You likely have heard the term "bloat," which refers to gastric torsion (gastric dilatation/volvulus), a potentially fatal condition in dogs that can affgect the Flat-Coated Retriever. The term *dilatation* means that the dog's stomach is filled with air, while *volvulus* means that the stomach is twisted around on itself, blocking the entrance/exit points. Dilatation/volvulus is truly a deadly combination, although they also can occur independently of each other. An affected dog cannot digest food or pass gas, and blood cannot flow to the stomach, causing accumulation of toxins and gas along with great pain and rapidily occuring shock.

Many theories exist on what exactly causes bloat, but we do know that deep-chested breeds are more prone. Activities like eating a large meal, gulping water, strenuous exercise too close to mealtimes or a combination of these factors can contribute to bloat, though not every case is directly related to these more well-known causes. With that in mind, we can focus on incorporating simple daily preventives and knowing how to recognize the symptoms; discuss these things with your veterinarian. Affected dogs need immediate veterinary attention, as death can result quickly. Signs include obvious restlessness/discomfort, crying in pain, drooling/excessive salivation, unproductive attempts to vomit or relieve himself, visibly bloated appearance and collapsing. Do not wait: get to the vet *right away* if you see any of these symptoms. The vet will confirm by x-ray if the stomach is bloated with air; if so, the dog must be treated *immediately*.

A bloated dog will be treated for shock, and the stomach must be relieved of the air pressure as well as surgically returned to its correct position. If part of the stomach wall has died, that part must be removed. Usually the stomach is stapled to the abdominal wall to prevent another episode of bloating; this may or may not be successful. The vet should also check the dog for heart problems, which can be side effects of bloat. As you can see, it's much easier and safer to prevent bloat than to treat it.

At this stage in your Flat-Coated Retriever's life, your veterinarian may want to schedule visits twice yearly, instead of once, to run some laboratory screenings, electrocardiograms and the like, and to change the diet to something more digestible. Catching problems early is the best way to manage them effectively. Treating the early stages of heart disease is so much easier than trying to intervene when there is more significant damage to the heart muscle.

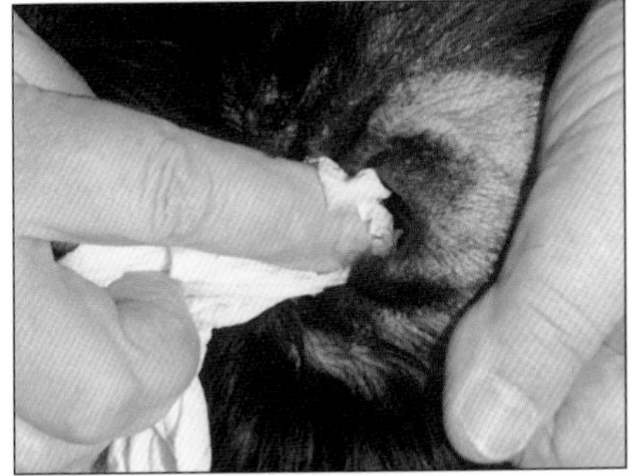

If your Flat-Coat swims frequently, as many do, the moisture in his ears many promote infections. Keep your dog's ears clean and dry, especially after each swim.

Similarly, managing the beginning of kidney problems is fairly routine if there is no significant kidney damage. Other problems,

Bloat-Prevention Tips

As varied as the causes of bloat are the tips for prevention, but some common preventive methods follow:

- Feed two or three small meals daily rather than one large one;
- Do not feed water before, after or with meals, but allow access to water at all other times;
- Never permit rapid eating or gulping of water;
- No exercise for the dog at least two hours before and (especially) after meals;
- Feed high-quality food with adequate protein, adequate fiber content and not too much fat and carbohydrate;
- Explore herbal additives, enzymes or gas-reduction products (only under a vet's advice) to encourage a "friendly" environment in the dog's digestive system;
- Avoid foods and ingredients known to produce gas;
- Avoid stressful situations for the dog, especially at mealtimes;
- Make dietary changes gradually, over a period of a few weeks;
- Do not feed dry food only;
- Although the role of genetics as a causative of bloat is not known, many breeders do not breed from previously affected dogs;
- Sometimes owners are advised to have gastroplexy (stomach stapling) performed on their dogs as a preventive measure.

Of utmost importance is that you know your dog! Pay attention to his behavior and any changes that could be symptomatic of bloat. Your dog's life depends on it!

like cognitive dysfunction (similar to senility and Alzheimer's disease), cancer, diabetes and arthritis, are more common in older dogs, but all can be treated to help the dog live as many happy, comfortable years as possible. Just as in people, medical management is more effective (and less expensive) when you catch things early.

SELECTING A VETERINARIAN

There is probably no more important decision that you will make regarding your pet's healthcare than the selection of his doctor. Your pet's veterinarian will be a pediatrician, family-practice physician and gerontologist, depending on the dog's life stage, and will be the individual who makes recommendations regarding issues such as when specialists need to be consulted, when diagnostic testing and/or therapeutic intervention is needed and when you will need to seek outside emergency and critical-care services. Your vet will act as your advocate and liaison throughout these processes.

Everyone has his own idea about what to look for in a vet, an individual who will play a big role in his dog's (and, of course, his own) life for many years to come. For some, it is the compassionate caregiver with whom they hope to develop a professional relationship to span the lifetime of their dogs and even their future pets. For others, they are seeking a clinician with keen diagnostic and therapeutic insight who can deliver state-of-the-art healthcare. Still others need a veterinary facility that is open evenings and weekends, is in close proximity or provides mobile veterinary services to accommodate their schedules; these people may not much mind that their dogs might see different veterinarians on each visit. Just as we have different reasons for selecting our own healthcare professionals (e.g., covered by insurance plan, expert in field, convenient location, etc.), we should not expect that there is a one-size-fits-all recommendation for selecting a veterinarian and veterinary practice. The best advice is to be honest in your assessment of what you expect from a veterinary practice and to conscientiously research the options in your area. You will quickly appreciate that not all veterinary practices are the same, and you will be happiest with one that truly meets your needs.

There is another point to be considered in the selection of veterinary services. Not that long ago, a single veterinarian would attempt to manage all medical and surgical issues as they arose. That was often problematic, because veterinarians are trained in many species and many diseases, and it was just impossible for general veterinary practitioners to be experts in every species, every field and every ailment. However, just as in the human healthcare fields, specialization has allowed general practitioners to concentrate on primary healthcare delivery, especially wellness and the prevention of infectious diseases, and to utilize a network of specialists to assist in the management of conditions that require specific expertise and experience. Thus there are now many types of veterinary specialists, including dermatologists, cardiologists, ophthalmologists, surgeons, internists, oncologists, neurologists, behaviorists, criticalists and others to help primary-care veterinarians deal with complicated medical challenges. In most cases, specialists see cases referred by primary-care veterinarians, make diagnoses and set up management plans. From there, the animals' ongoing care is returned to their primary-care veterinarians. This important team approach to your pet's medical-care needs has provided opportunities for advanced care and an unparalleled level of quality to be delivered.

With all of the opportunities for your Flat-Coated Retriever to receive high-quality veterinary medical care, there is another topic that needs to be addressed at the same time—cost. It's been said that you can have excellent

YOUR DOG NEEDS TO VISIT THE VET IF:

- He has ingested a toxin such as antifreeze or a toxic plant; in these cases, administer first aid and call the vet right away
- His teeth are discolored, loose or missing or he has sores or other signs of infection or abnormality in the mouth
- He has been vomiting, has had diarrhea or has been constipated for over 24 hours; call immediately if you notice blood
- He has refused food for over 24 hours
- His eating habits, water intake or toilet habits have noticeably changed; if you have noticed weight gain or weight loss
- He shows symptoms of bloat, which requires *immediate* attention
- He is salivating excessively
- He has a lump in his throat
- He has a lump or bumps anywhere on the body
- He is very lethargic
- He appears to be in pain or otherwise has trouble chewing or swallowing
- His skin loses elasticity

Of course, there will be other instances in which a visit to the vet is necessary; these are just some of the signs that could be indicative of serious problems that need to be caught as early as possible.

healthcare or inexpensive healthcare, but never both; this is as true in veterinary medicine as it is in human medicine. While veterinary costs are a fraction of what the same services cost in the human healthcare arena, it is still difficult to deal with unanticipated medical costs, especially since they can easily creep into hundreds or even thousands of dollars if specialists or emergency services become involved. However, there are ways of managing these risks. The easiest is to buy pet health insurance and realize that its foremost purpose is not to cover routine healthcare visits but rather to serve as an umbrella for those rainy days when your pet needs medical care and you don't want to worry about whether or not you can afford that care.

Pet insurance policies are very cost-effective (and very inexpensive by human health-insurance standards), but make sure that you buy the policy long before you intend to use it (preferably starting in puppyhood, because coverage will exclude pre-existing conditions) and that you are actually buying an indemnity insurance plan from an insurance company that is regulated by your state or province. Many insurance policy look-alikes are actually discount clubs that are redeemable only at specific locations and for specific services. An indemnity plan covers your pet at almost all veterinary, specialty and emergency practices and is an excellent way to manage your pet's ongoing healthcare needs.

Not every Flat-Coated Retriever requires the same healthcare. Each dog is an individual, and your vet will give you advice appropriate for your Flat-Coat.

VACCINATIONS AND INFECTIOUS DISEASES

There has never been an easier time to prevent a variety of infectious diseases in your dog, but the advances we've made in veterinary medicine come with a price—choice. While having these choices is a good thing, it also has never been more difficult for the pet owner (or the veterinarian) to make an informed decision about the best way to protect pets through vaccination.

Years ago, it was just accepted that puppies got a starter series of vaccinations and then annual "boosters" throughout their lives to keep them protected. As more and more vaccines became

Common Infectious Diseases

Let's discuss some of the diseases that create the need for vaccination in the first place. Following are the major canine infectious diseases and a simple explanation of each.

Rabies: A devastating viral disease that can be fatal in dogs and people. In fact, vaccination of dogs and cats is an important public-health measure to create a resistant animal buffer population to protect people from contracting the disease. Vaccination schedules are determined on a government level and are not optional for pet owners; rabies vaccination is required by law in all 50 states.

Parvovirus: A severe, potentially life-threatening disease that is easily transmitted between dogs. There are four strains of the virus, but it is believed that there is significant "cross-protection" between strains that may be included in individual vaccines.

Distemper: A potentially severe and life-threatening disease with a relatively high risk of exposure, especially in certain regions. In very high-risk distemper environments, young pups may be vaccinated with human measles vaccine, a related virus that offers cross-protection when administered at four to ten weeks of age.

Hepatitis: Caused by canine adenovirus type 1 (CAV-1), but since vaccination with the causative virus has a higher rate of adverse effects, cross-protection is derived from the use of adenovirus type 2 (CAV-2), a cause of respiratory disease and one of the potential causes of canine cough. Vaccination with CAV-2 provides long-term immunity against hepatitis, but relatively less protection against respiratory infection.

Canine cough: Also called tracheobronchitis, actually a fairly complicated result of viral and bacterial offenders; therefore, even with vaccination, protection is incomplete. Wherever dogs congregate, canine cough will likely be spread among them. Intranasal vaccination with *Bordetella* and parainfluenza is the best safeguard, but the duration of immunity does not appear to be very long, typically a year at most. These are non-core vaccines, but vaccination is sometimes mandated by boarding kennels, obedience classes, dog shows and other places where dogs congregate to try to minimize spread of infection.

Leptospirosis: A potentially fatal disease that is more common in some geographic regions. It is capable of being spread to humans. The disease varies with the individual "serovar," or strain, of *Leptospira* involved. Since there does not appear to be much cross-protection between serovars, protection is only as good as the likelihood that the serovar in the vaccine is the same as the one in the pet's local environment. Problems with *Leptospira* vaccines are that protection does not last very long, side effects are not uncommon and a large percentage of dogs (perhaps 30%) may not respond to vaccination.

Borrelia burgdorferi: The cause of Lyme disease, the risk of which varies with the geographic area in which the pet lives and travels. Lyme disease is spread by deer ticks in the eastern US and western black-legged ticks in the western part of the country, and the risk of exposure is high in some regions. Lameness, fever and inappetence are most commonly seen in affected dogs. The extent of protection from the vaccine has not been conclusively demonstrated.

Coronavirus: This disease has a high risk of exposure, especially in areas where dogs congregate, but it typically causes only mild to moderate digestive upset (diarrhea, vomiting, etc.). Vaccines are available, but the duration of protection is believed to be relatively short and the effectiveness of the vaccine in preventing infection is considered low.

There are many other vaccinations available, including those for *Giardia* and canine adenovirus-1. While there may be some specific indications for their use, and local risk factors to be considered, they are not widely recommended for most dogs.

Your Flat-Coat revels in his time outdoors, so let him enjoy it! Just be sure to check his skin and coat often for any signs of allergies, insect bites, parasites and other problems.

available, consumers wanted the convenience of having all of that protection in a single injection. The result was "multivalent" vaccines that crammed a lot of protection into a single syringe. The manufacturers' recommendations were to give the vaccines annually, and this was a simple enough protocol to follow. However, as veterinary medicine has become more sophisticated and we have started looking more at healthcare quandaries rather than convenience, it has become necessary to reevaluate the situation and deal with some tough questions. It is important to realize that whether or not to use a particular vaccine depends on the risk of contracting the disease against which it protects, the severity of the disease if it is contracted, the duration of immunity provided by the vaccine, the safety of the product and the needs of the individual animal. In a very general sense, rabies, distemper, hepatitis and parvovirus are considered core vaccine needs, while parainfluenza, *Bordetella bronchiseptica*, leptospirosis, coronavirus and borreliosis (Lyme disease) are considered non-core needs and best reserved for animals that demonstrate reasonable risk of contracting the diseases.

NEUTERING/SPAYING

Sterilization procedures (neutering for males/spaying for females) are meant to accomplish several purposes. While the underlying premise is to address the risk of pet overpopulation, there are also some medical and behavioral benefits to the surgeries as well. For females, spaying prior to the first estrus (heat cycle) leads to a marked reduction in the risk of mammary cancer. There also will be no manifestations of "heat" to attract male dogs and no bleeding in the house. For males, there is prevention of testicular cancer and a reduction in the risk of prostate problems. In both sexes, there may be some limited reduction in aggressive behaviors toward other dogs, and some diminishing of urine marking, roaming and mounting.

While neutering and spaying do indeed prevent animals from contributing to pet overpopulation, even no-cost and low-cost neutering options have not eliminated the problem. Perhaps one of the main reasons for this is that individuals who intentionally breed their dogs and those who allow their animals to run at large are the main causes of unwanted offspring. Also, animals in shelters are often there because they were abandoned or relinquished, not because they came from unplanned matings. Neutering/spaying is important, but it should be considered in the context of the real causes of animals' ending up in shelters and eventually being euthanized.

One of the important considerations regarding neutering is that it is a surgical procedure. This sometimes gets lost in discussions of low-cost procedures and commoditization of the process. In females, spaying is specifically referred to as an ovariohysterectomy. In this procedure, a midline incision is made in the abdomen and the entire uterus and both ovaries are surgically removed. While this is a major invasive surgical procedure, it usually has few complications, because it is typically performed on healthy young animals. However, it is major surgery, as any woman who has had a hysterectomy will attest.

In males, neutering has traditionally referred to castration, which involves the surgical removal of both testicles. While still a significant piece of surgery, there is not the abdominal exposure that is required in the female surgery. In addition, there is now a chemical sterilization option, in which a solution is injected into each testicle, leading to atrophy of the sperm-producing cells. This can typically be done under sedation rather than full anesthesia. This is a relatively new approach, and there are no long-term clinical studies yet available.

Neutering/spaying is typically done around six months of age at most veterinary hospitals, although techniques have been pioneered to perform the procedures in animals as young as eight weeks of age. In general, the surgeries on the very young animals are done for the specific reason of sterilizing them before they go to their new homes. This is done in some shelter hospitals for assurance that the animals will definitely not produce any pups. Otherwise, these organizations need to rely on owners to comply with their wishes to have the animals "altered" at a later date, something that does not always happen.

There are some exciting immunocontraceptive "vaccines" currently under development, and there may be a time when contraception in pets will not require surgical procedures. We anxiously await these developments.

HEREDITARY HEALTH CONCERNS FOR FLAT-COATS

Hereditary disease exists in most breeds of dog to some degree. The following problems can occur in the Flat-Coat. The frequency with which they affect individual dogs varies, but dedicated breeders work to keep their occurrence low.

Patellar Luxation

This is a condition in which the dog's kneecap will slip out of the joint and lock the leg straight. It can be surgically corrected to reduce pain and prevent recurrence, but affected dogs should be spayed or neutered. All breeding stock should be x-rayed and certified clear of this condition prior to consideration for breeding.

Hip Dysplasia (HD)

Hip dysplasia means, quite simply, poor or abnormal formation of the hip joint. It occurs most commonly in large breeds of dog and is known to be inherited. A severe case can render a hunting dog worthless in the field, and even a mild case can cause painful arthritis in the average house dog. Diagnosed only through x-ray examination by a veterinary radiologist, less severe cases may go undetected until the dog's mobility becomes impaired.

The trait is controlled by several recessive, polygenic genes, and dogs with non-dysplastic hips can carry recessive genes that will pass HD on to their progeny. Only by screening several generations of breeding stock can you be better assured of offspring with healthy hips.

While hip dysplasia is largely an inherited condition, research shows that environmental factors play a significant part in its development. Overfeeding and feeding a diet high in calories (primarily fat) during a puppy's rapid-growth stages are suspected to be contributing factors in the development of HD. Heavy-bodied and overweight puppies are more at risk than pups with very lean conformation.

Dogs 24 months of age and older should have their hips x-rayed and the x-rays evaluated to determine if any degree of dysplasia is present. The Orthopedic Foundation for Animals (OFA) evaluates x-rays and assigns each dog a grade based on their findings. Hip x-rays are submitted to the OFA, where they are reviewed by a panel of three board-certified veterinary radiologists. There are seven possible grades: Excellent, Good, Fair, Borderline, Mild, Moderate and Severe. Excellent, Good and Fair are considered normal and dogs with these gradings will receive an OFA number. The other four gradings do not warrant an OFA number, with the latter three indicating that the dog is affected by some level of dysplasia.

When visiting a litter, a

Do You Know about Hip Dysplasia?

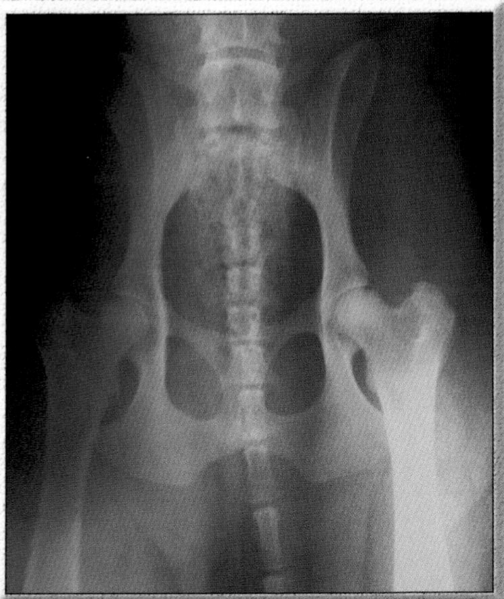

X-ray of a dog with "Good" hips.

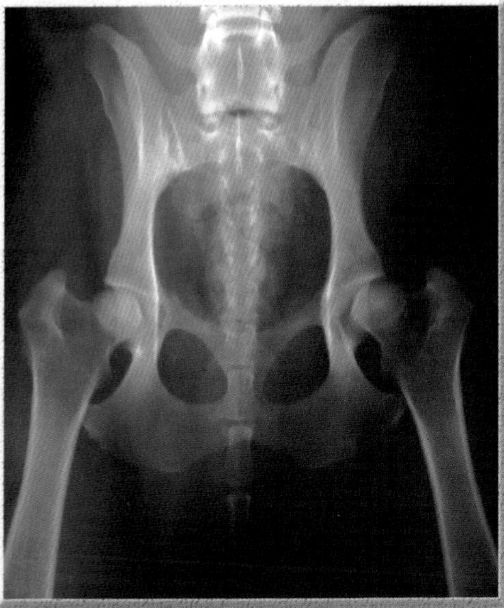

X-ray of a dog with "Moderate" dysplastic hips.

Hip dysplasia is a fairly common condition found in pure-bred dogs. When a dog has hip dysplasia, his hind leg has an incorrectly formed hip joint. By constant use of the hip joint, it becomes more and more loose, wears abnormally and may become arthritic.

Hip dysplasia can only be confirmed with an x-ray, but certain symptoms may indicate a problem. Your dog may have a hip dysplasia problem if he walks in a peculiar manner, hops instead of smoothly runs, uses his hind legs in unison (to keep the pressure off the weak joint), has trouble getting up from a prone position or always sits with both legs together on one side of his body.

As the dog matures, he may adapt well to life with a bad hip, but in a few years the arthritis develops and many dogs with hip dysplasia become crippled.

Hip dysplasia is considered an inherited disease and can be diagnosed definitively by x-ray only when the dog is two years old, although symptoms often appear earlier. Some experts claim that a special diet might help your puppy outgrow the bad hip, but the usual treatments are surgical. The removal of the pectineus muscle, the removal of the round part of the femur, reconstructing the pelvis and replacing the hip with an artificial one are all surgical interventions that are expensive, but they are usually very successful. Follow the advice of your veterinarian.

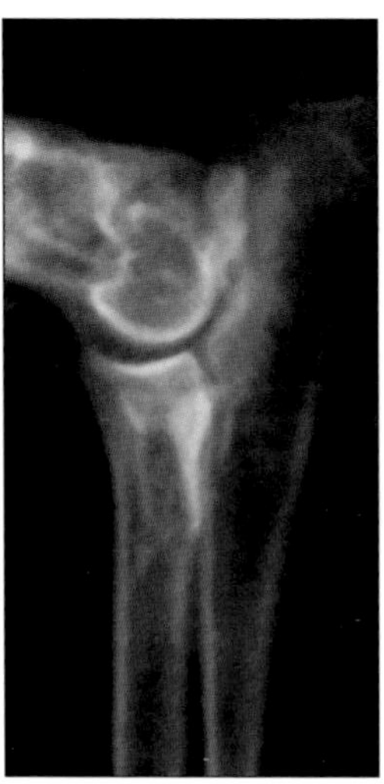

Elbow dysplasia as it appeared in a three-and-a-half year old dog.

potential owner should ask to see documentation of the litter's parents' hip clearances from OFA or another accredited organization; similar hip-testing schemes are in place in countries around the world. Good breeders have all of their breeding stock tested and only breed from those dogs and bitches who have received clearances.

Elbow Dysplasia (ED)

Elbow dysplasia is a developmental problem of the elbow joint, and large retriever breeds are frequently affected. While not a major problem in the Flat-Coated Retriever, some are known to be affected, and affected dogs should not be bred. The OFA offers an x-ray testing scheme for ED and other problems that can affect the elbow.

Epilepsy

Epilepsy is evidenced by seizures resulting from abnormal brain activity. Seizures vary in frequency and severity from dog to dog, but it is thought that epilepsy has a genetic basis and thus affected dogs should be excluded from breeding programs. Seizures can have serious consequences, but they can be controlled by medication, allowing an epileptic dog to live a normal life.

Hypothyroidism

Hypothyroidism is a complex metabolic disease associated with malfunction of the thyroid gland. Some Flat-Coated Retrievers may be prone to low thyroid levels, which can cause obesity, poor coat condition, hair loss, allergies and reproductive problems. Fortunately, it is not widespread within the breed and is easily managed when it occurs.

Cancer

Cancer has become a serious problem in this breed, and can be a problem in many breeds. The age of onset appears to be about four years of age, with several forms of cancer claiming victims. Research is ongoing, and prospective owners should inquire about the occurrence of cancer in the lines of the puppy or dog under consideration. Discovery of any lumps, bumps or other external abnormalities anywhere on your Flat-Coat certainly requires veterinary attention. Many cancers, though, cannot be seen or felt, so screening and watching for symptoms are essential for early detection; discuss this with your vet.

Breeders strive to breed only dogs with no hereditary problems, thereby producing healthy dogs and decreasing the occurrence of inherited health problems.

S. E. M. by Dr. Dennis Kunkel, University of Hawaii

A scanning electron micrograph of a dog flea, *Ctenocephalides canis*, on dog hair.

EXTERNAL PARASITES

Fleas

Fleas have been around for millions of years and, while we have better tools now for controlling them than at any time in the past, there still is little chance that they will end up on an endangered species list. Actually, they are very well adapted to living on our pets, and they continue to adapt as we make advances.

The female flea can consume 15 times her weight in blood during active reproduction and can lay as many as 40 eggs a day. These eggs are very resistant to the effects of insecticides. They hatch into larvae, which then mature and spin cocoons. The immature fleas reside in this pupal stage until the time is right for feeding. This pupal stage is also very resistant to the effects of insecticides, and pupae can last in the environment without feeding for many months. Newly emergent fleas are attracted to animals by the warmth of the animals' bodies, movement and exhaled carbon dioxide. However, when they first emerge from their cocoons, they orient towards light; thus when an animal passes between a flea and the light source, casting a shadow, the flea pounces and starts to feed. If the animal turns out to be a dog or cat, the reproductive cycle continues. If the flea lands on another type of animal, including a person, the flea will bite but will then look for a more appropriate host. An emerging adult flea can survive without feeding for up to 12 months but, once it tastes blood, it can survive off its host for only three to four days.

It was once thought that fleas spend most of their lives in the environment, but we now know that fleas won't willingly jump off a dog unless leaping to another dog or when physically removed by brushing, bathing or other manipulation. Flea eggs, on the other hand, are shiny and smooth, and they roll off the animal and into the environment. The eggs, larvae and pupae then exist in the environment, but once the adult finds a susceptible animal, it's home sweet home until the flea is forced to seek refuge elsewhere.

Since adult fleas live on the animal and immature forms survive in the environment, a successful treatment plan must address all stages of the flea life cycle. There are now several safe and effective flea-control products that can be applied on a monthly basis. These include fipronil, imidacloprid, selamectin and permethrin (found in several formulations). Most of these products have significant flea-killing rates within 24 hours. However, none of them will control the immature forms in the environment. To accomplish this, there are a variety of insect growth regulators that can be

FLEA PREVENTION FOR YOUR DOG

- Discuss with your veterinarian the safest product to protect your dog, likely in the form of a monthly tablet or a liquid preparation placed on the back of the dog's neck.
- For dogs suffering from flea-bite dermatitis, a shampoo or topical insecticide treatment is required.
- Your lawn and property should be sprayed with an insecticide designed to kill fleas and ticks that lurk outdoors.
- Using a flea comb, check the dog's coat regularly for any signs of parasites.
- Practice good housekeeping. Vacuum floors, carpets and furniture regularly, especially in the areas that the dog frequents, and wash the dog's bedding weekly.
- Follow up house-cleaning with carpet shampoos and sprays to rid the house of fleas at all stages of development. Insect growth regulators are the safest option.

THE FLEA'S LIFE CYCLE

What came first, the flea or the egg? This age-old mystery is more difficult to comprehend than the actual cycle of the flea. Fleas usually live only about four months. A female can lay 2,000 eggs in her lifetime.

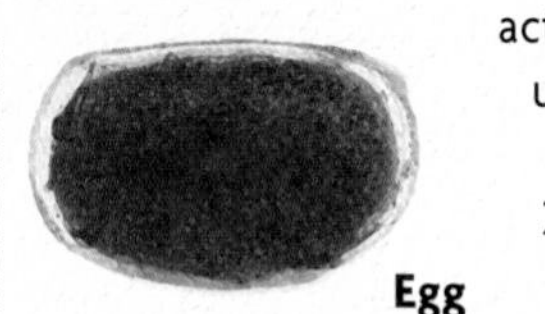

Egg

Photo by Carolina Biological Supply Co.

After ten days of rolling around your carpet or under your furniture, the eggs hatch into larvae, which feed on various and sundry debris. In days or months, depending on the climate, the larvae spin cocoons and develop into the pupal or nymph stage, which quickly develop into fleas.

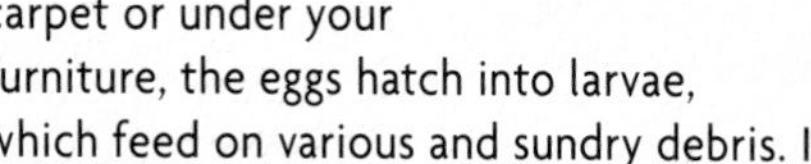

Larva

Photo by Carolina Biological Supply Co.

Pupa

These immature fleas must locate a host within 10 to 14 days or they will die. Only about 1% of the flea population exist as adult fleas, while the other 99% exist as eggs, larvae or pupae.

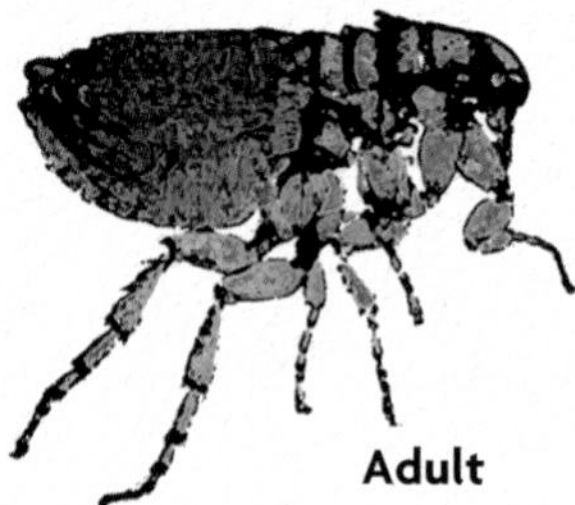

Adult

KILL FLEAS THE NATURAL WAY

If you choose not to go the route of conventional medication, there are some natural ways to ward off fleas:

- Dust your dog with a natural flea powder, composed of such herbal goodies as rosemary, wormwood, pennyroyal, citronella, rue, tobacco powder and eucalyptus.
- Apply diatomaceous earth, the fossilized remains of single-cell algae, to your carpets, furniture and pet's bedding. Even though it's not good for dogs, it's even worse for fleas, which will dry up swiftly and die.
- Brush your dog frequently, give him adequate exercise and let him fast occasionally. All of these activities strengthen the dog's system and make him more resistant to disease and parasites.
- Bathe your dog with a capful of pennyroyal or eucalyptus oil.
- Feed a natural diet, free of additives and preservatives. Add some fresh garlic and brewer's yeast to the dog's morning portion, as these items have flea-repelling properties.

sprayed into the environment (e.g., pyriproxyfen, methoprene, fenoxycarb) as well as insect development inhibitors such as lufenuron that can be administered. These compounds have no effect on adult fleas, but they stop immature forms from developing into adults. In years gone by, we relied heavily on toxic insecticides (such as organophosphates, organochlorines and carbamates) to manage the flea problem, but today's options are not only much safer to use on our pets but also safer for the environment.

TICKS

Ticks are members of the spider class (arachnids) and are blood-sucking parasites capable of transmitting a variety of diseases, including Lyme disease, ehrlichiosis, babesiosis and Rocky Mountain spotted fever. It's easy to see ticks on your own skin, but it is more of a challenge when your furry companion is affected. Whenever you happen to be planning a stroll in a tick-infested area (especially forests, grassy or wooded areas or parks) be prepared to do a thorough inspection of your dog afterward to search for ticks. Ticks can be tricky, so make sure you spend time looking in the ears, between the toes and everywhere else where a tick might hide. Ticks need to be attached for 24–72 hours before they transmit most of the diseases that they carry, so you do have a window of opportunity for some preventive intervention.

A TICKING BOMB

There is nothing good about a tick's harpooning his nose into your dog's skin. Among the diseases caused by ticks are Rocky Mountain spotted fever, canine ehrlichiosis, canine babesiosis, canine hepatozoonosis and Lyme disease. If a dog is allergic to the saliva of a female wood tick, he can develop tick paralysis.

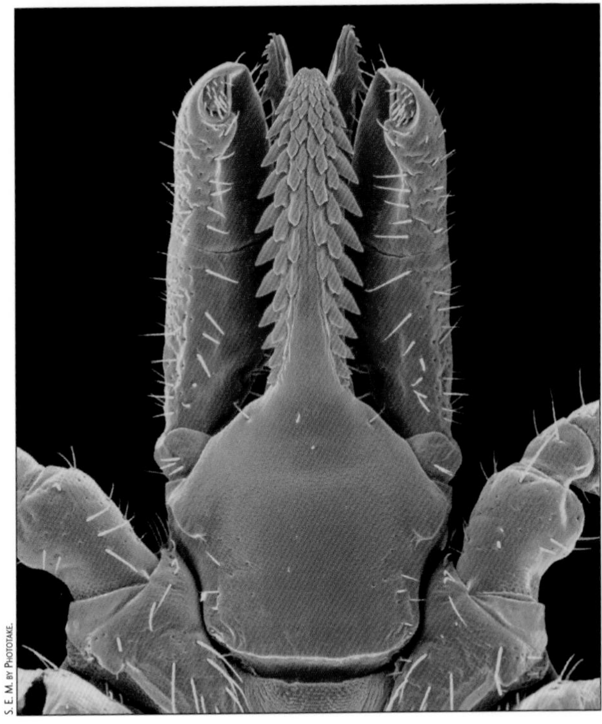

S. E. M. BY PHOTOTAKE.

A scanning electron micrograph of the head of a female deer tick, *Ixodes dammini*, a parasitic tick that carries Lyme disease.

Female ticks live to eat and breed. They can lay between 4,000 and 5,000 eggs and they die soon after. Males, on the other hand, live only to mate with the females and continue the process as long as they are able. Most ticks live on multiple hosts before parasitizing dogs. The immature forms typically reside on grass and shrubs, waiting for susceptible animals to walk by. The larvae and nymph stages typically feed on wildlife.

If only a few ticks are present on a dog, they can be plucked out, but it is important to remove the entire head and mouthparts,

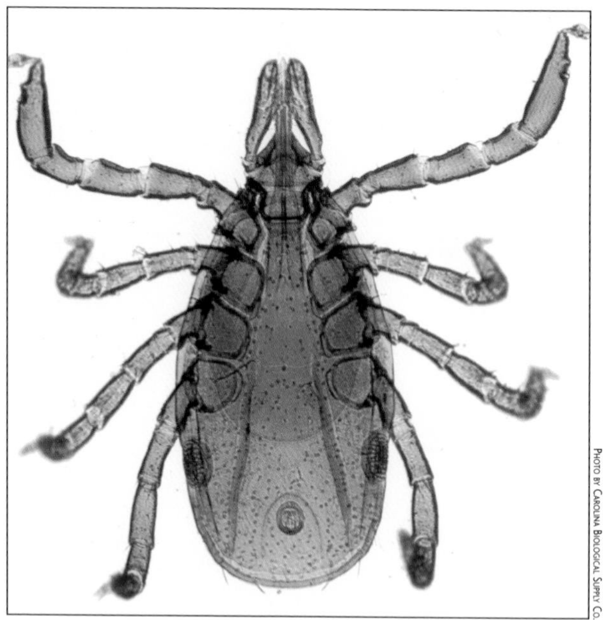
Photo by Carolina Biological Supply Co.

Deer tick, *Ixodes dammini.*

which may be deeply embedded in the skin. This is best accomplished with forceps designed especially for this purpose; fingers can be used but should be protected with rubber gloves, plastic wrap or at least a paper towel. The tick should be grasped as closely as possible to the animal's skin and should be pulled upward with steady, even pressure. Do not squeeze, crush or puncture the body of the tick or you risk exposure to any disease carried by that tick. Once the ticks have been removed, the sites of attachment should be disinfected. Your hands should then be washed with soap and water to further minimize risk of contagion. The tick should be disposed of in a container of alcohol or household bleach.

Some of the newer flea products, specifically those with fipronil, selamectin and permethrin, have effect against some, but not all, species of tick. Flea collars containing appropriate pesticides (e.g., propoxur, chlorfenvinphos) can aid in tick control. In most areas, such collars should be placed on animals in March, at the beginning of the tick season, and changed regularly. Leaving the collar on when the pesticide level is waning invites the development of resistance. Amitraz collars are also good for tick control, and the active ingredient does not interfere with other flea-control products. The ingredient helps prevent the attachment of ticks to the skin and will cause those ticks already on the skin to detach themselves.

TICK CONTROL

Removal of underbrush and leaf litter and the thinning of trees in areas where tick control is desired are recommended. These actions remove the cover and food sources for small animals that serve as hosts for ticks. With continued mowing of grasses in these areas, the probability of ticks' surviving is further reduced. A variety of insecticide ingredients (e.g., resmethrin, carbaryl, permethrin, chlorpyrifos, dioxathion and allethrin) are registered for tick control around the home.

MITES

Mites are tiny arachnid parasites that parasitize the skin of dogs. Skin diseases caused by mites are referred to as "mange," and there are many different forms seen in dogs. These forms are very different from one another, each one warranting an individual description.

Sarcoptic mange, or scabies, is one of the itchiest conditions that affects dogs. The microscopic *Sarcoptes* mites burrow into the superficial layers of the skin and can drive dogs crazy with itchiness. They are also communicable to people, although they can't complete their reproductive cycle on people. In addition to being tiny, the mites also are often difficult to find when trying to make a diagnosis. Skin scrapings from multiple areas are examined microscopically but, even then, sometimes the mites cannot be found.

Fortunately, scabies is relatively easy to treat, and there are a variety of products that will successfully kill the mites. Since the mites can't live in the environment for very long without feeding, a complete cure is usually possible within four to eight weeks.

Cheyletiellosis is caused by a relatively large mite, which sometimes can be seen even without a microscope. Often referred to as "walking dandruff," this also causes itching, but not usually as profound as with scabies.

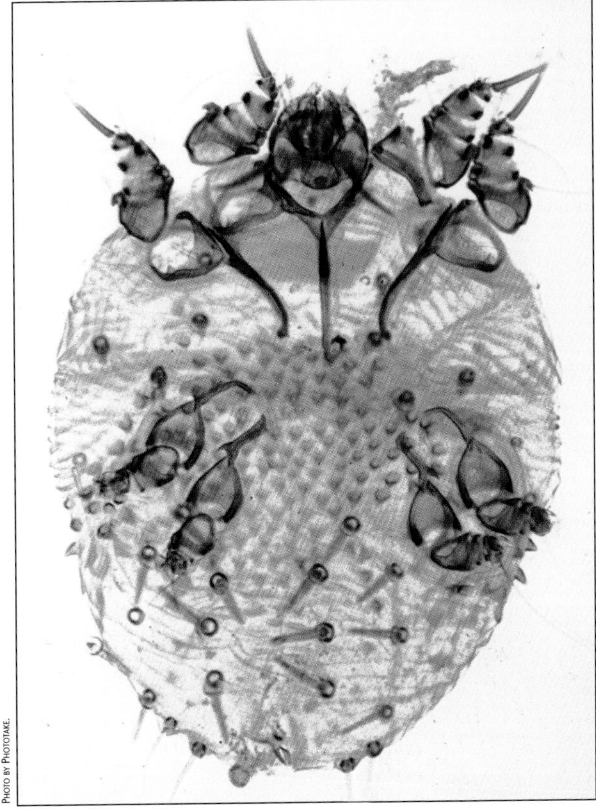

PHOTO BY PHOTOTAKE.

***Sarcoptes scabiei*, commonly known as the "itch mite."**

While *Cheyletiella* mites can survive somewhat longer in the environment than scabies mites, they too are relatively easy to treat, being responsive to not only the medications used to treat scabies but also often to flea-control products.

Otodectes cynotis is the canine ear mite and is one of the more common causes of mange, especially in young dogs in shelters or pet stores. That's because the mites are typically present in large numbers and are quickly spread to

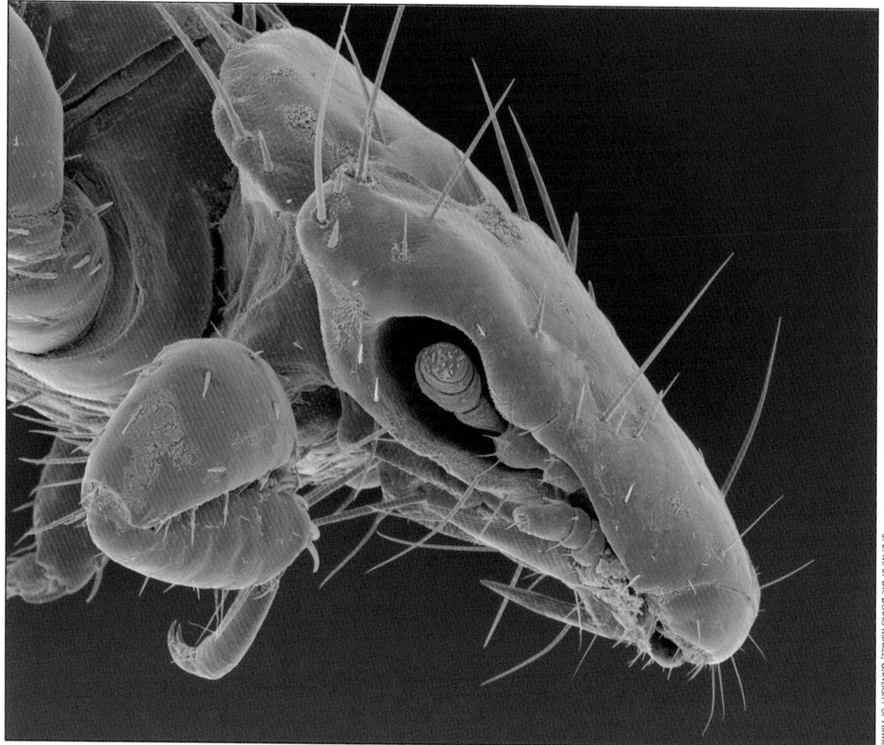

Micrograph of a dog louse, ***Heterodoxus spiniger***. Female lice attach their eggs to the hairs of the dog. As the eggs hatch, the larval lice bite and feed on the blood. Lice can also feed on dead skin and hair. This feeding activity can cause hair loss and skin problems.

S. E. M. by Dr. Dennis Kunkel, University of Hawaii.

nearby animals. The mites rarely do much harm but can be difficult to eradicate if the treatment regimen is not comprehensive. While many try to treat the condition with ear drops only, this is the most common cause of treatment failure. Ear drops cause the mites to simply move out of the ears and as far away as possible (usually to the base of the tail) until the insecticide levels in the ears drop to an acceptable level—then it's back to business as usual! The successful treatment of ear mites requires treating all animals in the household with a systemic insecticide, such as selamectin, or a combination of miticidal ear drops combined with whole-body flea-control preparations.

Demodicosis, sometimes referred to as red mange, can be one of the most difficult forms of mange to treat. Part of the problem has to do with the fact that the mites live in the hair follicles and they are relatively well shielded from topical and systemic products. The main issue, however, is that demodectic mange typically results only when there is some underlying process interfering with the dog's immune system.

Since *Demodex* mites are

normal residents of the skin of mammals, including humans, there is usually a mite population explosion only when the immune system fails to keep the number of mites in check. In young animals, the immune deficit may be transient or may reflect an actual inherited immune problem. In older animals, demodicosis is usually seen only when there is another disease hampering the immune system, such as diabetes, cancer, thyroid problems or the use of immune-suppressing drugs. Accordingly, treatment involves not only trying to kill the mange mites but also discerning what is interfering with immune function and correcting it if possible.

Chiggers represent several different species of mite that don't parasitize dogs specifically, but do latch on to passersby and can cause irritation. The problem is most prevalent in wooded areas in the late summer and fall. Treatment is not difficult, as the mites do not complete their life cycle on dogs and are susceptible to a variety of miticidal products.

MOSQUITOES

Mosquitoes have long been known to transmit a variety of diseases to people, as well as just being biting pests during warm weather. They also pose a real risk to pets. Not only do they carry deadly heartworms but recently there also has been much concern over their involvement with West Nile virus. While we can avoid heartworm with the use of preventive medications, there are no such preventives for West Nile virus. The only method of prevention in endemic areas is active mosquito control. Fortunately, most dogs that have been exposed to the virus only developed flu-like symptoms and, to date, there have not been the large number of reported deaths in canines as seen in some other species.

ILLUSTRATION BY PHOTOTAKE

Illustration of *Demodex folliculoram.*

MOSQUITO REPELLENT

Low concentrations of DEET (less than 10%), found in many human mosquito repellents, have been safely used in dogs but, in these concentrations, probably give only about two hours of protection. DEET may be safe in these small concentrations, but since it is not licensed for use on dogs, there is no research proving its safety for dogs. Products containing permethrin give the longest-lasting protection, perhaps two to four weeks. As DEET is not licensed for use on dogs, and both DEET and permethrin can be quite toxic to cats, appropriate care should be exercised. Other products, such as those containing oil of citronella, also have some mosquito-repellent activity, but typically have a relatively short duration of action.

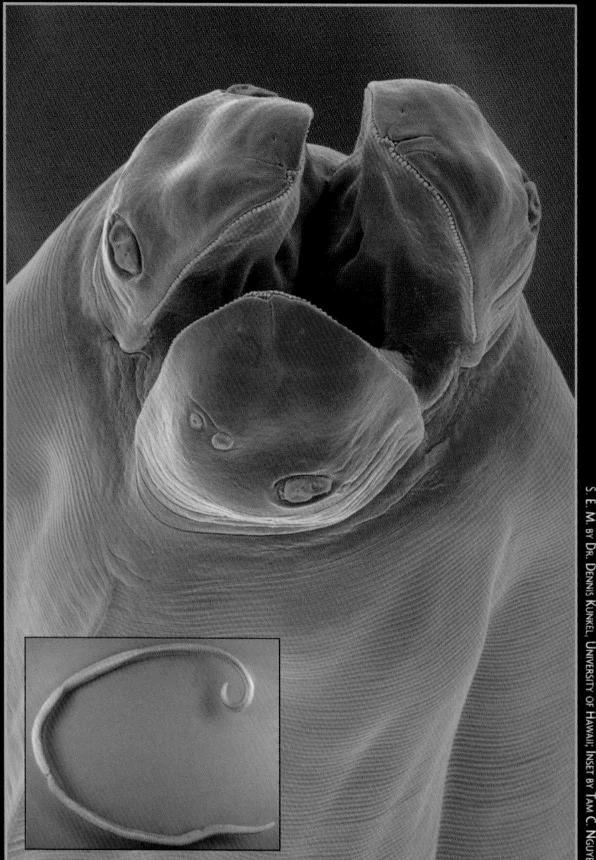

S. E. M. by Dr. Dennis Kunkel, University of Hawaii; Inset by Tam C. Nguyen.

ASCARID DANGERS

The most commonly encountered worms in dogs are roundworms known as ascarids. *Toxascaris leonine* and *Toxocara canis* are the two species that infect dogs. Subsisting in the dog's stomach and intestines, adult roundworms can grow to 7 inches in length and adult females can lay in excess of 200,000 eggs in a single day.

In humans, visceral larval migrans affects people who have ingested eggs of *Toxocara canis*, which frequently contaminates children's sandboxes, beaches and park grounds. The roundworms reside in the human's stomach and intestines, as they would in a dog's, but do not mature. Instead, they find their way to the liver, lungs and skin, or even to the heart or kidneys in severe cases. Deworming puppies is critical in preventing the infection in humans, and young children should never handle nursing pups who have not been dewormed.

The ascarid roundworm *Toxocara canis*, showing the mouth with three lips. INSET: Photomicrograph of the roundworm *Ascaris lumbricoides*.

INTERNAL PARASITES: WORMS

Ascarids

Ascarids are intestinal roundworms that rarely cause severe disease in dogs. Nonetheless, they are of major public health significance because they can be transferred to people. Sadly, it is children who are most commonly affected by the parasite, probably from inadvertently ingesting ascarid-contaminated soil. In fact, many yards and children's sandboxes contain appreciable numbers of ascarid eggs. So, while ascarids don't bite dogs or latch onto their intestines to suck blood, they do cause some nasty medical conditions in children and are best eradicated from our furry friends. Because pups can start passing ascarid eggs by three weeks of age, most parasite-control programs begin at two weeks of age and are repeated every two weeks until pups are eight weeks old. It is important to

HOOKED ON *ANCYLOSTOMA*

Adult dogs can become infected by the bloodsucking nematodes we commonly call hookworms via ingesting larvae from the ground or via the larvae penetrating the dog's skin. It is not uncommon for infected dogs to show no symptoms of hookworm infestation. Sometimes symptoms occur within ten days of exposure. These symptoms can include bloody diarrhea, anemia, loss of weight and general weakness. Dogs pass the hookworm eggs in their stools, which serves as the vet's method of identifying the infestation. The hookworm larvae can encyst themselves in the dog's tissues and be released when the dog is experiencing stress.

Caused by an *Ancylostoma* species whose common host is the dog, cutaneous larval migrans affects humans, causing itching and lumps and streaks beneath the surface of the skin.

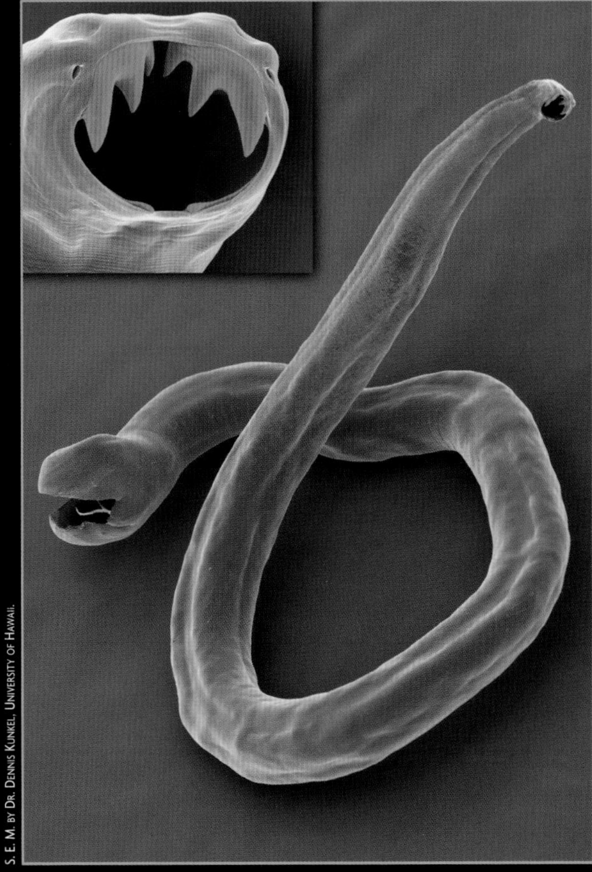

S. E. M. BY DR. DENNIS KUNKEL, UNIVERSITY OF HAWAII.

The hookworm *Ancylostoma caninum* infests the intestines of dogs. INSET: Note the row of hooks at the posterior end, used to anchor the worm to the intestinal wall.

realize that bitches can pass ascarids to their pups even if they test negative prior to whelping. Accordingly, bitches are best treated at the same time as the pups.

HOOKWORMS

Unlike ascarids, hookworms do latch onto a dog's intestinal tract and can cause significant loss of blood and protein. Similar to ascarids, hookworms can be transmitted to humans, where they cause a condition known as cutaneous larval migrans. Dogs can become infected either by consuming the infective larvae or by the larvae's penetrating the skin directly. People most often get infected when they are lying on the ground (such as on a beach) and the larvae penetrate the skin. Yes, the larvae can penetrate through a beach blanket. Hookworms are typically susceptible to the same medications used to treat ascarids.

Whipworms

Whipworms latch onto the lower aspects of the dog's colon and can cause cramping and diarrhea. Eggs do not start to appear in the dog's feces until about three months after the dog was infected. This worm has a peculiar life cycle, which makes it more difficult to control than ascarids or hookworms. The good thing is that whipworms rarely are transferred to people.

Some of the medications used to treat ascarids and hookworms are also effective against whipworms, but, in general, a separate treatment protocol is needed. Since most of the medications are effective against the adults but not the eggs or larvae, treatment is typically repeated in three weeks, and then often in three months as well. Unfortunately, since dogs don't develop resistance to whipworms, it is difficult to prevent them from getting reinfected if they visit soil contaminated with whipworm eggs.

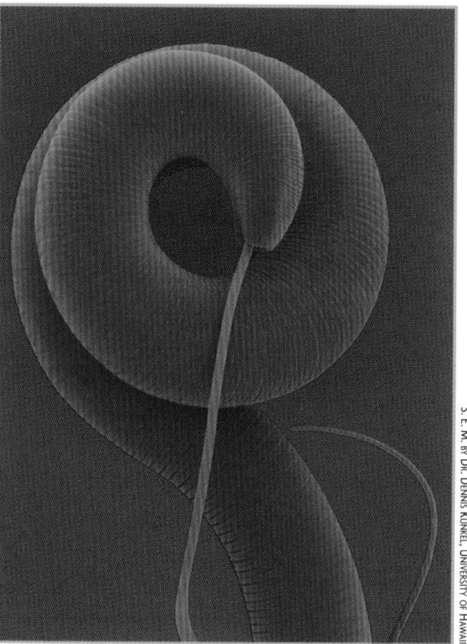

Adult whipworm, *Trichuris* sp., an intestinal parasite.

S.E.M. by Dr. Dennis Kunkel, University of Hawaii.

WORM-CONTROL GUIDELINES

- Practice sanitary habits with your dog and home.
- Clean up after your dog and don't let him sniff or eat other dogs' droppings.
- Control insects and fleas in the dog's environment. Fleas, lice, cockroaches, beetles, mice and rats can act as hosts for various worms.
- Prevent dogs from eating uncooked meat, raw poultry and dead animals.
- Keep dogs and children from playing in sand and soil.
- Kennel dogs on cement or gravel; avoid dirt runs.
- Administer heartworm preventives regularly.
- Have your vet examine your dog's stools at your annual visits.
- Select a boarding kennel carefully so as to avoid contamination from other dogs or an unsanitary environment.
- Prevent dogs from roaming. Obey local leash laws.

Tapeworms

There are many different species of tapeworm that affect dogs, but *Dipylidium caninum* is probably the most common and is spread by fleas. Flea larvae feed on organic debris and tapeworm eggs in the environment and, when a dog chews at himself and manages to ingest fleas, he might get a dose of tapeworm at the same time. The tapeworm then develops further in the intestine of the dog.

The tapeworm itself, which is a parasitic flatworm that latches onto the intestinal wall, is composed of numerous segments. When the segments break off into the intestine (as proglottids), they may accumulate around the rectum, like grains of rice. While this tapeworm is disgusting in its behavior, it is not directly communicable to humans (although humans can also get infected by swallowing fleas).

S. E. M. by Dr. Dennis Kunkel, University of Hawaii.

A dog tapeworm proglottid (body segment).

A much more dangerous flatworm is *Echinococcus multilocularis*, which is typically found in foxes, coyotes and wolves. The eggs are passed in the feces and infect rodents, and, when dogs eat the rodents, the dogs can be infected by thousands of adult tapeworms. While the parasites don't cause many problems in dogs, this is considered the most lethal worm infection that people can get. Take appropriate precautions if you live in an area in which these tapeworms are found. Do not use mulch that may contain feces of dogs, cats or wildlife, and discourage your pets from hunting wildlife. Treat these tapeworm infections aggressively in pets, because if humans get infected, approximately half die.

Heartworms

Heartworm disease is caused by the parasite *Dirofilaria immitis* and is seen in dogs around the world. A member of the roundworm group, it is spread between dogs by the bite of an infected mosquito. The mosquito injects infective larvae into the dog's skin with its bite, and these larvae develop under the skin for a period of time before making their way to the heart. There they develop into adults, which grow and create blockages of the heart, lungs and major blood vessels there. They also start producing offspring (microfilariae)

S. E. M. by Dr. Dennis Kunkel, University of Hawaii.

The dog tapeworm *Taenia pisiformis.*

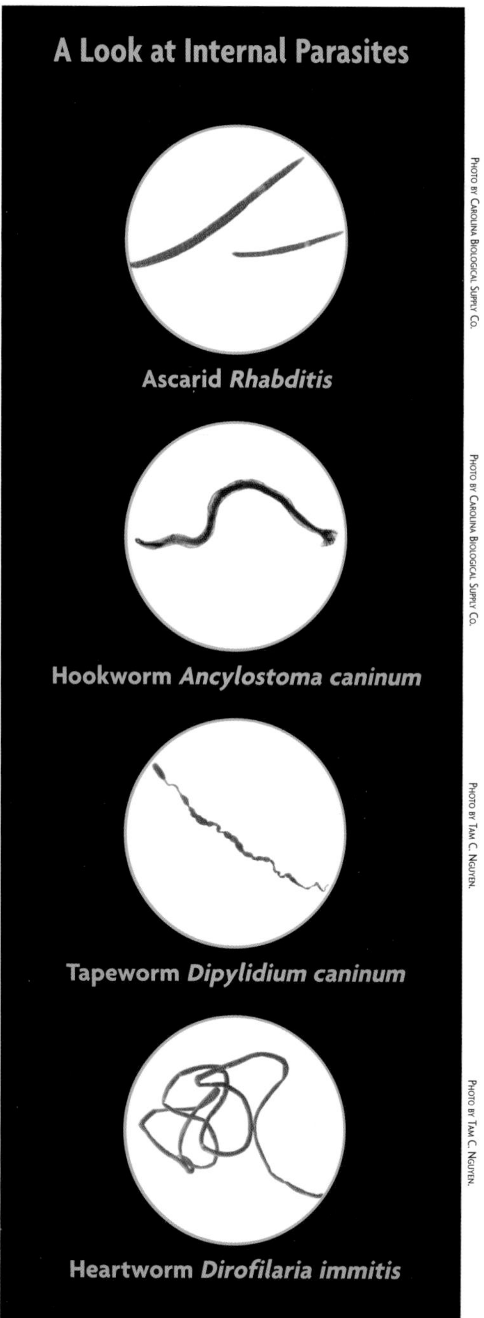

A Look at Internal Parasites

Ascarid *Rhabditis*

Photo by Carolina Biological Supply Co.

Hookworm *Ancylostoma caninum*

Photo by Carolina Biological Supply Co.

Tapeworm *Dipylidium caninum*

Photo by Tam C. Nguyen.

Heartworm *Dirofilaria immitis*

Photo by Tam C. Nguyen.

and these microfilariae circulate in the bloodstream, waiting to hitch a ride when the next mosquito bites. Once in the mosquito, the microfilariae develop into infective larvae and the entire process is repeated.

When dogs get infected with heartworm, over time they tend to develop symptoms associated with heart disease, such as coughing, exercise intolerance and potentially many other manifestations. Diagnosis is confirmed by either seeing the microfilariae themselves in blood samples or using immunologic tests (antigen testing) to identify the presence of adult heartworms. Since antigen tests measure the presence of adult heartworms and microfilarial tests measure offspring produced by adults, neither are positive until six to seven months after the initial infection. However, the beginning of damage can occur by fifth-stage larvae as early as three months after infection. Thus it is possible for dogs to be harboring problem-causing larvae for up to three months before either type of test would identify an infection.

The good news is that there are great protocols available for preventing heartworm in dogs. Testing is critical in the process, and it is important to understand the benefits as well as the limitations of such testing. All dogs six months of age or older that have not been on continuous heartworm-preventive medication

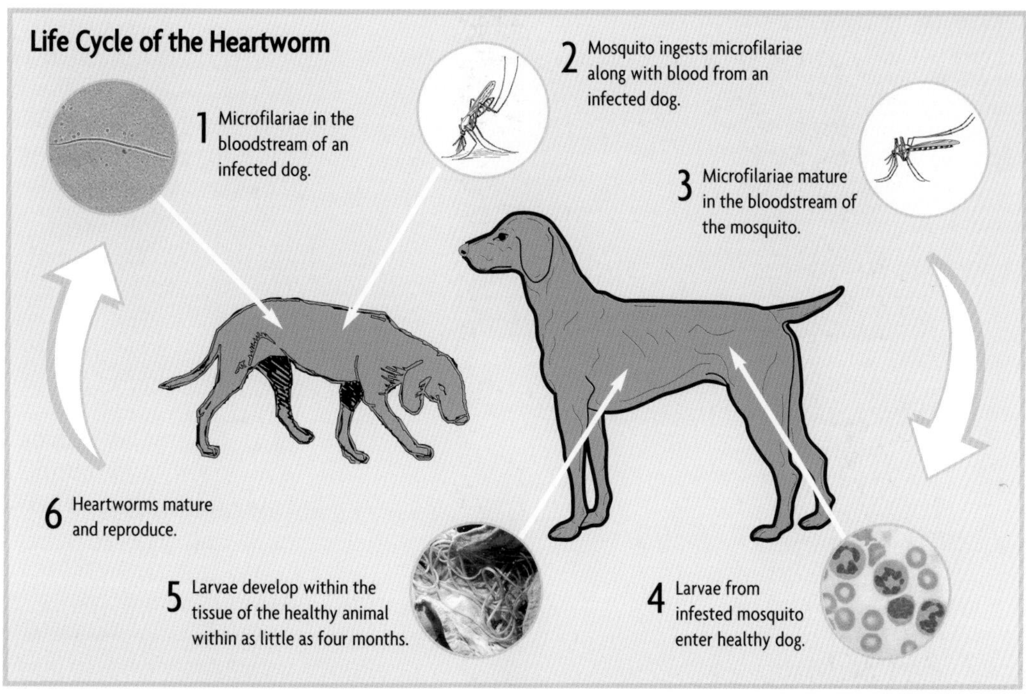

should be screened with microfilarial or antigen tests. For dogs receiving preventive medication, periodic antigen testing helps assess the effectiveness of the preventives. The American Heartworm Society guidelines suggest that annual retesting may not be necessary when owners have absolutely provided continuous heartworm prevention. Retesting on a two- to three-year interval may be sufficient in these cases. However, your veterinarian will likely have specific guidelines under which heartworm preventives will be prescribed, and many prefer to err on the side of safety and retest annually.

It is indeed fortunate that heartworm is relatively easy to prevent, because treatments can be as life-threatening as the disease itself. Treatment requires a two-step process that kills the adult heartworms first and then the microfilariae. Prevention is obviously preferable; this involves a once-monthly oral or topical treatment. The most common oral preventives include ivermectin (not suitable for some breeds), moxidectin and milbemycin oxime; the once-a-month topical drug selamectin provides heartworm protection in addition to flea, tick and other parasite controls.

Owners and breeders are looking for Flat-Coated Retrievers with clear, healthy eyes.

A PET OWNER'S GUIDE TO COMMON OPHTHALMIC DISEASES

BY PROF. DR. ROBERT L. PEIFFER, JR.

Few would argue that vision is the most important of the cognitive senses, and maintenance of a normal visual system is important for an optimal quality of life. Likewise, pet owners tend to be acutely aware of their pets' eyes and vision, which is important because early detection of ocular disease will optimize therapeutic outcomes. The eye is a sensitive organ with minimal reparative capabilities, and with some diseases, such as glaucoma, uveitis and retinal detachment, early diagnosis and treatment can be critical in terms of whether vision can be preserved.

The causes of ocular disease are quite varied; the nature of dogs makes them susceptible to traumatic conditions, the most common of which include proptosis of the globe, cat scratch injuries and penetrating wounds from foreign objects, including sticks and air-rifle pellets. Infectious diseases caused by bacteria, viruses or fungi may be localized to the eye or part of a systemic infection. Many of the common conditions, including eyelid conformational problems, cataracts, glaucoma and retinal degenerations, have a genetic basis.

Before acquiring your puppy, it is important to ascertain that both parents have been examined and certified as free of eye disease by a veterinary ophthalmologist. Since many of these genetic diseases can be detected early in life, acquire the pup on the condition that it pass a thorough ophthalmic examination by a qualified specialist.

Lower entropion, or rolling in of the eyelid, is causing irritation in the left eye of this young dog. Several extra eyelashes, or distichiasis, are present on the lower lid.

LID CONFORMATIONAL ABNORMALITIES

Rolling in (entropion) or out (ectropion) of the lids tends to be a breed-related problem. Entropion can involve the upper and/or lower lids. Signs usually appear between 3 and 12 months of age. The irritation caused by the eyelid hairs' rubbing

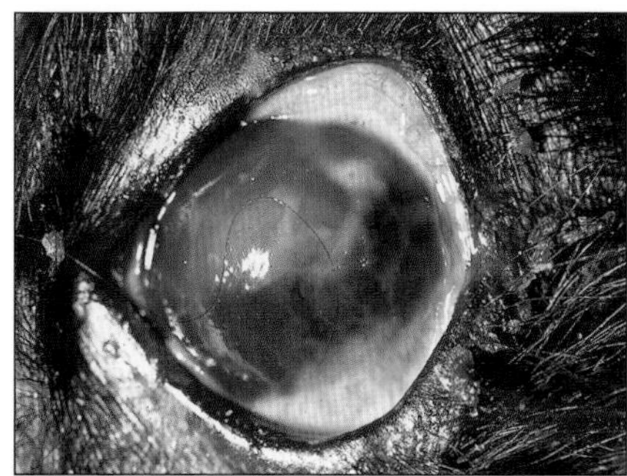

Keratoconjunctivitis sicca, seen here in the right eye of a middle-aged dog, causes a characteristic thick mucous discharge as well as secondary corneal changes.

on the surface of the cornea may result in blinking, tearing and damage to the cornea. Ectropion is likewise breed-related and is considered "normal" in hounds, for instance; unlike entropion, which results in acute discomfort, ectropion may cause chronic irritation related to exposure and the pooling of secretions. Most of these cases can be managed medically with daily irrigation with sterile saline and topical antibiotics when required.

Eyelash Abnormalities

Dogs normally have lashes only on the upper lids, in contrast to humans. Occasionally extra eyelashes may be seen emerging at the eyelid margin (distichiasis) or through the inner surface of the eyelid (ectopic cilia).

Conjunctivitis

Inflammation of the conjunctiva, the pink tissue that lines the lids and the anterior portion of the sclera, is generally accompanied by redness, discharge and mild discomfort. The majority of cases are associated with either bacterial infections or dry eye syndrome. Fortunately, topical medications are generally effective in curing or controlling the problem.

Dry Eye Syndrome

Dry eye syndrome (keratoconjunctivitis sicca) is a common cause of external ocular disease. Discharge is typically thick and sticky, and keratitis is a frequent component; any breed can be affected. While some cases can be associated with toxic effects of drugs, including the sulfa antibiotics, the cause in the majority of the cases cannot be determined and is assumed to be immune-mediated.

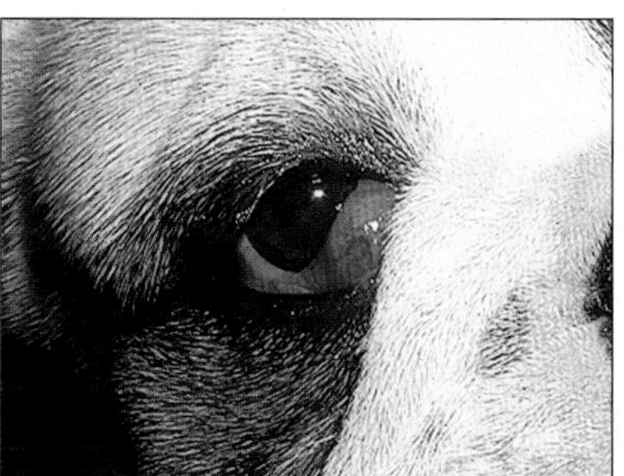

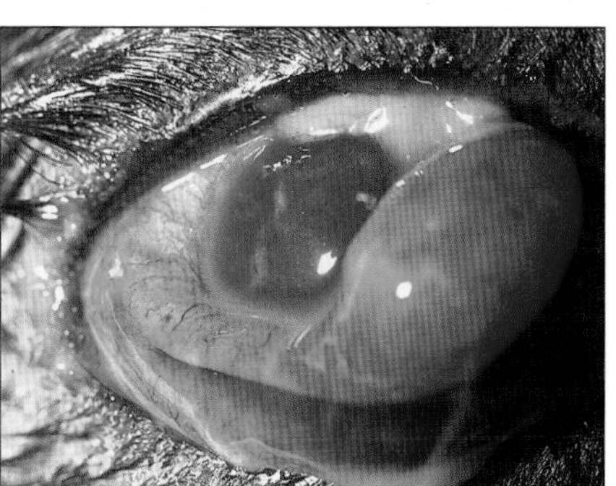

LEFT: Prolapse of the gland of the third eyelid in the right eye of a pup. RIGHT: In this case, in the right eye of a young dog, the prolapsed gland can be seen emerging between the edge of the third eyelid and the corneal surface.

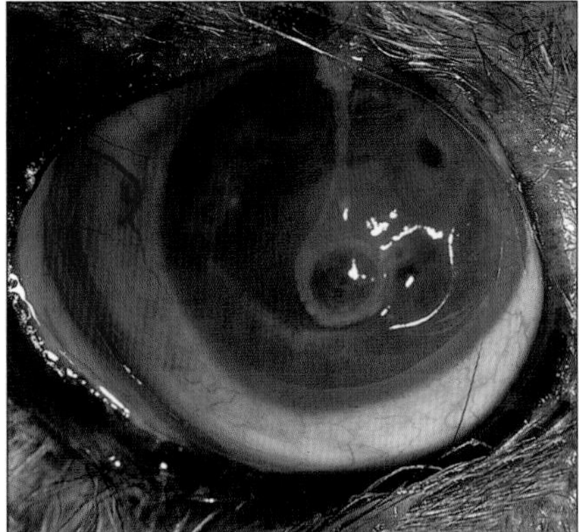

Multiple deep ulcerations affect the cornea of this middle-aged dog.

Prolapse of the Gland of the Third Eyelid

In this condition, commonly referred to as *cherry eye*, the gland of the third eyelid, which produces about one-third of the aqueous phase of the tear film and is normally situated within the anterior orbit, prolapses to emerge as a pink fleshy mass protruding over the edge of the third eyelid, between the third eyelid and the cornea. The condition usually develops during the first year of life and, while mild irritation may result, the condition is unsightly as much as anything else.

Corneal Disease

The cornea is the clear front part of the eye that provides the first step in the collection of light on its journey to be eventually focused onto the retina, and most corneal diseases will be manifested by alterations in corneal transparency. The cornea is an exquisitely innervated tissue, and defects in corneal integrity are accompanied by pain, which is demonstrated by squinting.

Corneal ulcers may occur secondarily to trauma or to irritation from entropion or ectopic cilia. In middle-aged or older dogs, epithelial ulcerations may occur spontaneously due to an inherent defect; these are referred to as indolent or Boxer ulcers, in recognition of the breed in which we see the condition most frequently. Infection may occur secondarily. Ulcers can be potentially blinding conditions; severity is dependent upon the size and depth of the ulcer and other complicating features.

Non-ulcerative keratitis tends to have an immune-mediated component and is managed by topical immunosuppressants, usually corticosteroids. Corneal edema can occur in elderly dogs. It is due to a failure of the corneal endothelial "pump."

The cornea responds to chronic irritation by transforming

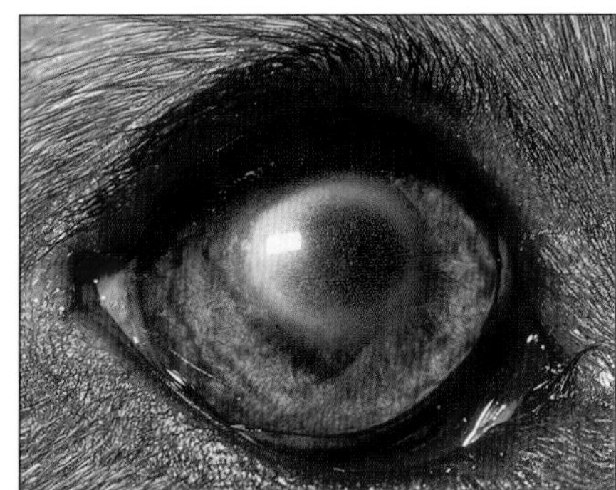

Lipid deposition can occur as a primary inherited dystrophy, or secondarily to hypercholesterolemia (in dogs frequently associated with hypothyroidism), chronic corneal inflammation or neoplasia. The deposits in this dog assume an oval pattern in the center of the cornea.

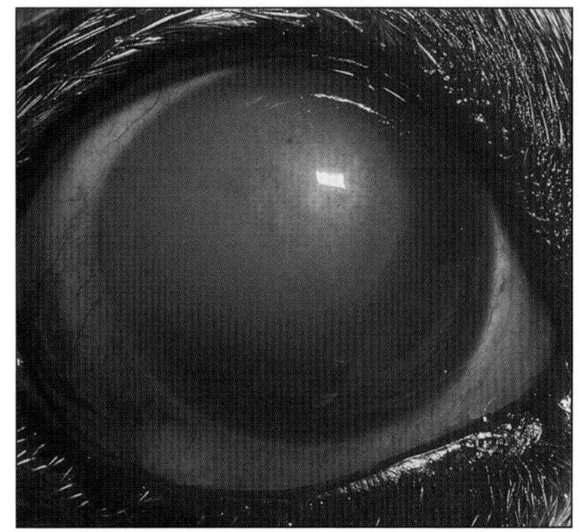

ABOVE LEFT & RIGHT: Corneal edema can develop as a slowly progressive process in elderly Boston Terriers, Miniature Dachshunds and Miniature Poodles, as well as others, as a result of the inability of the corneal endothelial "pump" to maintain a state of dehydration.

into skin-like tissue that is evident clinically by pigmentation, scarring and vascularization; some cases may respond to tear stimulants, lubricants and topical corticosteroids, while others benefit from surgical narrowing of the eyelid opening in order to enhance corneal protection.

Uveitis

Inflammation of the vascular tissue of the eye—the uvea—is a common and potentially serious disease in dogs. While it may occur secondarily to trauma or other intraocular diseases, such as cataracts, most commonly uveitis is associated with some type of systemic infectious or neoplastic process. Uncontrolled, uveitis can lead to blinding cataracts, glaucoma and/or retinal detachments, and aggressive symptomatic therapy with dilating agents (to prevent pupillary adhesions) and anti-inflammatories is critical.

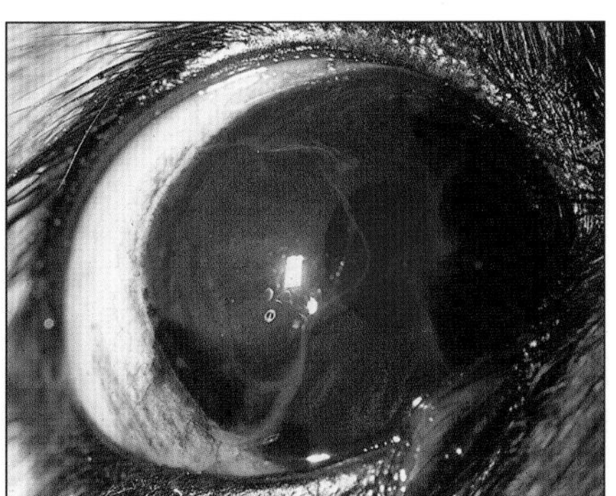

Medial pigmentary keratitis in this dog is associated with irritation from prominent facial folds.

Glaucoma

The eye is essentially a hollow fluid-filled sphere, and the pressure within is maintained by regulation of the rate of fluid production and fluid egress at 10–20 mms of mercury. The retinal cells are extremely sensitive to elevations of intraocular pressure and, unless controlled, permanent blindness can occur within hours to days. In acute glaucoma, the conjunctiva becomes congested, the cornea cloudy, the pupil moderate and fixed; the eye is generally painful and avisual. Increased constant signs of

Glaucoma in the dog most commonly occurs as a sudden extreme elevation of intraocular pressure, frequently to three to four times the norm. The eye of this dog demonstrates the common signs of episcleral injection, or redness; mild diffuse corneal cloudiness, due to edema; and a mid-sized fixed pupil.

discomfort will accompany chronic cases.

Management of glaucoma is one of the most challenging situations the veterinary ophthalmologist faces; in spite of intense efforts, many of these cases will result in blindness. Glaucoma has emerged in the Flat-Coat in the UK, where testing and research are ongoing.

Cataracts and Lens Dislocation

Cataracts are the most common blinding condition in dogs; fortunately, they are readily amenable to surgical intervention, with excellent results in terms of restoration of vision and replacement of the cataractous lens with a synthetic one. Most cataracts in dogs are inherited; less commonly cataracts can be secondary to trauma or other ocular diseases, including uveitis, glaucoma, lens luxation and retinal degeneration, or secondary to an underlying systemic metabolic disease, including diabetes and Cushing's disease. Signs include a progressive loss of the bright dark appearance of the pupil, which is replaced by a blue-gray hazy appearance. In this respect, cataracts need to be distinguished from the normal aging process of nuclear sclerosis, which occurs in middle-aged or older animals, and has minimal effect on vision.

Lens dislocation occurs in dogs and frequently leads to secondary glaucoma; early removal of the dislocated lens is generally curative.

Retinal Disease

Retinal degenerations are usually inherited but may be associated

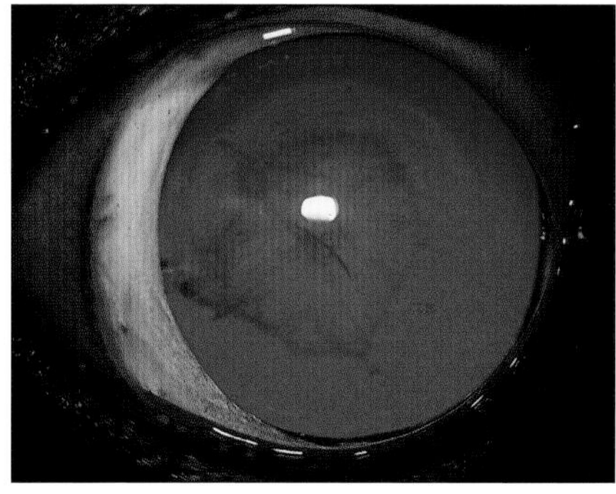

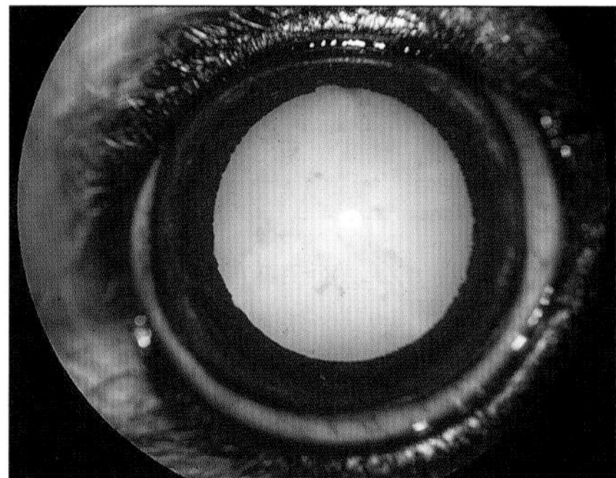

LEFT: The typical posterior subcapsular cataract appears between one and two years of age, but rarely progresses to where the animal has visual problems. RIGHT: Inherited cataracts generally appear between three and six years of age, and progress to the stage seen where functional vision is significantly impaired.

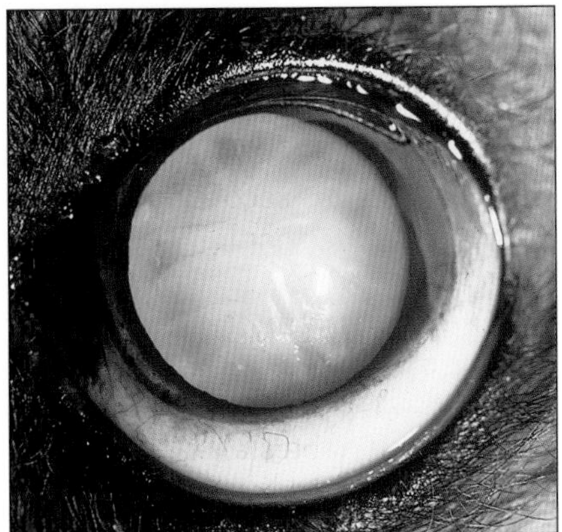

Anterior lens luxation can occur as a primary disease in the terrier breeds, or secondarily to trauma. The fibers that hold the lens in place rupture and the lens may migrate through the pupil to be situated in front of the iris. Secondary glaucoma is a frequent and significant complication that can be avoided if the dislocated lens is removed surgically.

with vitamin E deficiency in dogs. While signs are variable, most frequently one notes a decrease in vision over a period of months, which typically starts out as a night blindness. The cause of a more rapid loss of vision due to retinal degeneration occurs over days to weeks is labeled sudden acquired retinal degeneration or SARD; the outcome, however, is unfortunately usually similar to inherited and nutritional conditions, as the retinal tissues possess minimal regenerative capabilities. Most pets, however, with a bit of extra care and attention, show an amazing ability to adapt to an avisual world, and can be maintained as pets with a satisfactory quality of life. Detachment of the retina—due to accumulation of blood between the retina and the underlying uvea, which is called the *choroid*—can occur secondarily to retinal tears or holes, tractional forces within the eye, or as a result of uveitis. These types of detachments may be amenable to surgical repair if diagnosed early.

Optic Nerve

Optic neuritis, or inflammation of the nerve that connects the eye with the brain stem, is a relatively uncommon condition that occurs usually with rather sudden loss of vision and widely dilated non-responsive pupils.

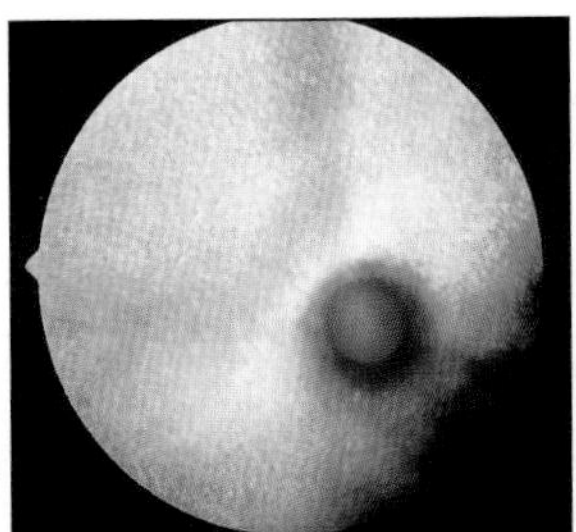

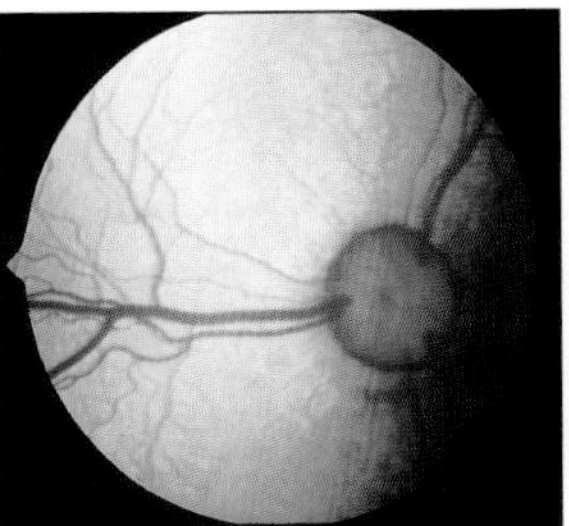

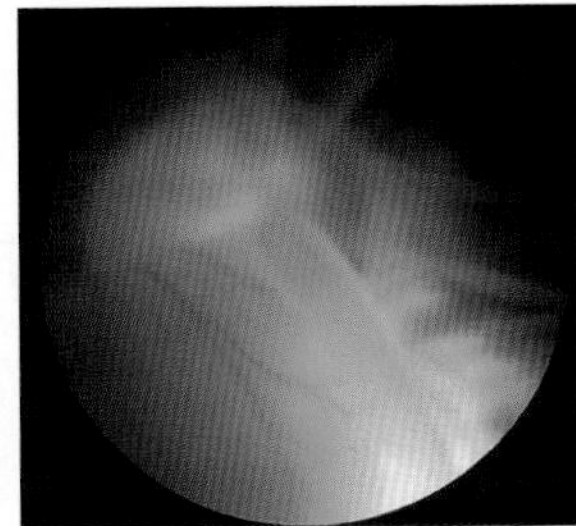

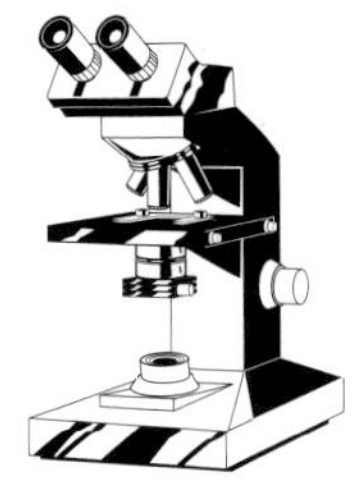

LEFT: The posterior pole of a normal fundus is shown; prominent are the head of the optic nerve and the retinal blood vessels. The retina is transparent, and the prominent green tapetum is seen superiorly.
CENTER: An eye with inherited retinal dysplasia is depicted. The tapetal retina superior to the optic disc is disorganized, with multifocal areas of hyperplasia of the retinal pigment epithelium.
RIGHT: Severe collie eye anomaly and a retinal detachment; this eye is unfortunately blind.

THE ABCs OF Emergency Care

Abrasions
Clean wound with running water or 3% hydrogen peroxide. Pat dry with gauze and spray with antibiotic. Do not cover.

Animal Bites
Clean area with soap and saline solution or water. Apply pressure to any bleeding area. Apply antibiotic ointment.

Antifreeze Poisoning
Induce vomiting and take dog to the vet.

Bee Sting
Remove stinger and apply soothing lotion or cold compress; give antihistamine in proper dosage.

Bleeding
Apply pressure directly to wound with gauze or towel for five to ten minutes. If wound does not stop bleeding, wrap wound with gauze and adhesive tape.

Bloat/Gastric Torsion
Immediately take the dog to the vet or emergency clinic; phone from car. No time to waste.

Burns
Chemical: Bathe dog with water and pet shampoo. Rinse in saline solution. Apply antibiotic ointment.

Acid: Rinse with water. Apply one part baking soda, two parts water to affected area.

Alkali: Rinse with water. Apply one part vinegar, four parts water to affected area.

Electrical: Apply antibiotic ointment. Seek veterinary assistance immediately.

Choking
If the dog is on the verge of collapsing, wedge a solid object, such as the handle of screwdriver, between molars on one side of the mouth to keep mouth open. Pull tongue out. Use long-nosed pliers or fingers to remove foreign object. Do not push the object down the dog's throat. For small or medium dogs, hold dog upside down by hind legs and shake firmly to dislodge foreign object.

Chlorine Ingestion
With clean water, rinse the mouth and eyes. Give the dog water to drink; contact the vet.

Constipation
Feed dog 2 tablespoons bran flakes with each meal. Encourage drinking water. Mix 1/4 teaspoon mineral oil in dog's food.

Diarrhea
Withhold food for 12 to 24 hours. Feed dog antidiarrheal with eyedropper. When feeding resumes, feed one part boiled hamburger, one part plain cooked rice, 1/4 to 3/4 cup four times daily.

Dog Bite
Snip away hair around puncture wound; clean with 3% hydrogen peroxide; apply tincture of iodine. If wound appears deep, take the dog to the vet.

Frostbite
Wrap the dog in a heavy blanket. Warm affected area with a warm bath for ten minutes. Red color to skin will return with circulation; if tissues are pale after 20 minutes, contact the vet.

Use a portable, durable container large enough to contain all items

Heat Stroke
Partially submerge the dog in cold water to lower his body temperature while contacting the veterinarian.

Hot Spots
Mix 2 packets Domeboro® with 2 cups water. Saturate cloth with mixture and apply to hot spots for 15 to 30 minutes. Apply antibiotic ointment. Repeat every six to eight hours.

Poisonous Plants
Wash affected area with soap and water. Cleanse with alcohol. For foxtail/grass, apply antibiotic ointment.

Rat Poison Ingestion
Induce vomiting. Keep dog calm, maintain dog's normal body temperature (use blanket or heating pad). Get to the vet for antidote.

Shock
Keep the dog calm and warm; call for veterinary assistance.

Snake Bite
If possible, bandage the area and apply pressure. If the area is not conducive to bandaging, use ice to control bleeding. Get immediate help from the vet.

Tick Removal
Apply flea and tick spray directly on tick. Wait one minute. Using tweezers or wearing plastic gloves, apply constant pull while grasping tick's body. Apply antibiotic ointment.

Vomiting
Restrict dog's water intake; offer a few ice cubes. Withhold food for next meal. Contact vet if vomiting persists longer than 24 hours.

DOG OWNER'S FIRST-AID KIT

- ❑ Gauze bandages/swabs
- ❑ Adhesive and non-adhesive bandages
- ❑ Antibiotic powder
- ❑ Antiseptic wash
- ❑ Hydrogen peroxide 3%
- ❑ Antibiotic ointment
- ❑ Lubricating jelly
- ❑ Rectal thermometer
- ❑ Nylon muzzle
- ❑ Scissors and forceps
- ❑ Eyedropper
- ❑ Syringe
- ❑ Anti-bacterial/fungal solution
- ❑ Saline solution
- ❑ Antihistamine
- ❑ Cotton balls
- ❑ Nail clippers
- ❑ Screwdriver/pen knife
- ❑ Flashlight
- ❑ Emergency phone numbers

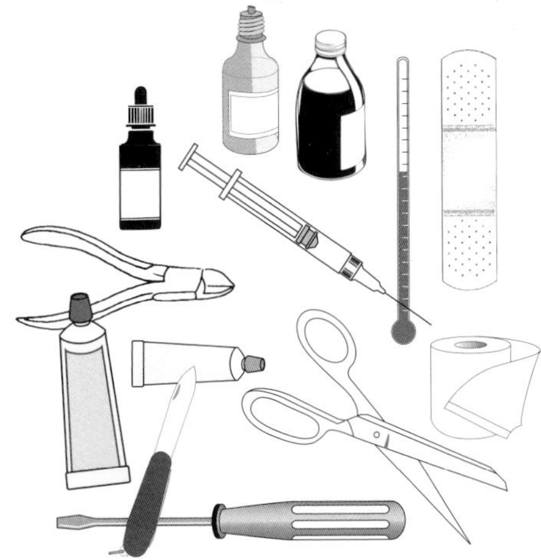

Number-One Killer Disease in Dogs: CANCER

In every age, there is a word associated with a disease or plague that causes humans to shudder. In the 21st century, that word is "cancer." Just as cancer is the leading cause of death in humans, it claims nearly half the lives of dogs that die from a natural disease as well as half the dogs that die over the age of ten years.

Described as a genetic disease, cancer becomes a greater risk as the dog ages. Vets and dog owners have become increasingly aware of the threat of cancer to dogs. Statistics reveal that one dog in every five will develop cancer, the most common of which is skin cancer. Many cancers, including prostate, ovarian and breast cancer, can be avoided by spaying and neutering our dogs by the age of six months.

Early detection of cancer can save or extend a dog's life, so it is absolutely vital for owners to have their dogs examined by a qualified vet or oncologist immediately upon detection of any abnormality. Certain dietary guidelines have also proven to reduce the onset and spread of cancer. Foods based on fish rather than beef, due to the presence of Omega-3 fatty acids, are recommended. Other amino acids such as glutamine have significant benefits for canines, particularly those breeds that show a greater susceptibility to cancer.

Cancer management and treatments promise hope for future generations of canines. Since the disease is genetic, breeders should never breed a dog whose parents, grandparents and any related siblings have developed cancer. It is difficult to know whether to exclude an otherwise healthy dog from a breeding program, as the disease usually does not manifest itself until the dog's adult years.

RECOGNIZE CANCER WARNING SIGNS

Since early detection can possibly rescue your dog from becoming a cancer statistic, it is essential for owners to recognize the possible signs and seek the assistance of a qualified professional.

- Abnormal bumps or lumps that continue to grow
- Bleeding or discharge from any body cavity
- Persistent stiffness or lameness
- Recurrent sores or sores that do not heal
- Inappetence
- Breathing difficulties
- Weight loss
- Bad breath or odors
- General malaise and fatigue
- Eating and swallowing problems
- Difficulty urinating and defecating

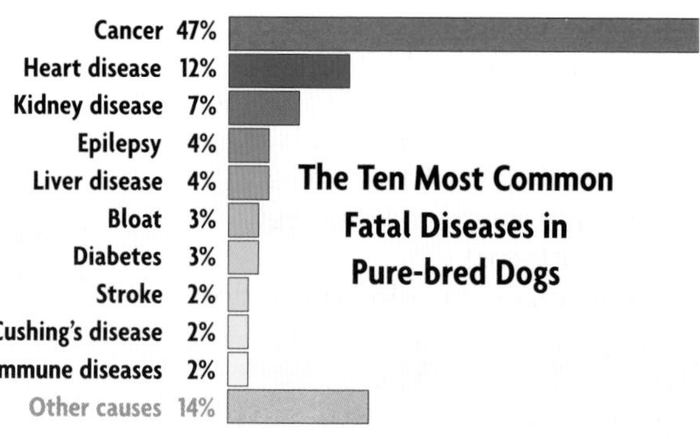

The Ten Most Common Fatal Diseases in Pure-bred Dogs

FLAT-COATED RETRIEVER

When we bring home a puppy, full of the energy and exuberance that accompanies youth, we hope for a long, happy and fulfilling relationship with the new family member. Even when we adopt an older dog, we look forward to the years of companionship ahead with a new canine friend. However, aging is inevitable for all creatures, and there will come a time when your Flat-Coated Retriever reaches his senior years and will need special considerations and attention to his care.

WHEN IS MY DOG A "SENIOR"?

In general, purebred dogs are considered to have achieved senior status when they reach 75% of their breed's average lifespan, with lifespan being generally based on breed size along with breed specific factors. Your Flat-Coat is a senior citizen at around 7, with an average lifespan of 10–12 years, although some have lived well into their teens!

Obviously, the old "seven dog years to one human year" theory is not exact. In puppyhood, a dog's year is actually comparable to more than seven human years, considering the puppy's rapid growth during his first year. Then, in adulthood, the ratio decreases. Regardless, the more viable rule of thumb is that the larger the dog, the shorter his expected lifespan. Of course, this can vary among individual dogs, with many living longer than expected, which we hope is the case!

ACCIDENT ALERT!

Just as we puppy-proof our homes for the new member of the family, we must accident-proof our homes for the older dog. You want to create a safe environment in which the senior dog can get around easily and comfortably, with no dangers. A dog that slips and falls in old age is much more prone to injury than an adult, making accident prevention even more important. Likewise, dogs are more prone to falls in old age, as they do not have the same balance and coordination that they once had. Throw rugs on hardwood floors are slippery and pose a risk; even a throw rug on a carpeted surface can be an obstacle for the senior dog. Consider putting down non-slip surfaces or confining your dog to carpeted rooms.

WHAT ARE THE SIGNS OF AGING?

By the time your dog has reached his senior years, you will know him very well, so the physical and behavioral changes that accompany aging should be noticeable to you. Humans and dogs share the most obvious physical sign of aging: gray hair! Graying often occurs first on the muzzle and face, around the eyes. Other telltale signs are the dog's overall decrease in activity. Your older dog might be more content to nap and rest, and he may not show the same old enthusiasm when it's time to play in the yard or go for a walk. Other physical signs include significant weight loss or gain; more labored movement; skin and coat problems, possibly hair loss; sight and/or hearing problems; changes in toileting habits, perhaps seeming "unhousebroken" at times; tooth decay, bad breath or other mouth problems.

There are behavioral changes that go along with aging, too. There are numerous causes for behavioral changes. Sometimes a dog's apparent confusion results from a physical change like diminished sight or hearing. If his confusion causes him to be afraid, he may act aggressively or defensively. He may sleep more frequently because his daily walks, though shorter now, tire him out. He may begin to experience separation anxiety or, conversely, become less interested in petting and attention.

There also are clinical conditions that cause behavioral changes in older dogs. One such condition is known as canine cognitive dysfunction (familiarly known as "old-dog" syndrome). It can be frustrating for an owner whose dog is affected with cognitive dysfunction, as it can result in behavioral changes of all types, most seemingly unexplainable. Common changes include the

ADAPTING TO AGE

As dogs age and their once-keen senses begin to deteriorate, they can experience stress and confusion. However, dogs are very adaptable, and most can adjust to deficiencies in their sight and hearing. As these processes often deteriorate gradually, the dog makes adjustments gradually, too. Because dogs become so familiar with the layout of their homes and yards, and with their daily routines, they are able to get around even if they cannot see or hear as well. Help your senior dog by keeping things consistent around the house. Keep up with your regular times for walking and potty trips, and do not relocate his crate or rearrange the furniture. Your dog is a very adaptable creature and can make compensation for his diminished ability, but you want to help him along the way and not make changes that will cause him confusion.

WEATHER WORRIES

Older pets are less tolerant of extremes in weather, both heat and cold. Your older dog should not spend extended periods in the sun; when outdoors in the warm weather, make sure he does not become overheated. In chilly weather, consider a sweater for your dog when outdoors and limit time spent outside. Whether or not his coat is thinning, he will need provisions to keep him warm when the weather is cold. You may even place his bed by a heating duct in your living room or bedroom.

dog's forgetting aspects of the daily routine, such as times to eat, go out for walks, relieve himself and the like. Along the same lines, you may take your dog out at the regular time for a potty trip and he may have no idea why he is there. Sometimes a placid dog will begin to show aggressive or possessive tendencies or, conversely, a hyperactive dog will start to "mellow out."

Disease also can be the cause of behavioral changes in senior dogs. Hormonal problems (Cushing's disease is common in older dogs), diabetes and thyroid disease can cause increased appetite, which can lead to aggression related to food guarding. It's better to be proactive with your senior dog, making more frequent trips to the vet if necessary and having bloodwork done to test for the diseases that can commonly befall older dogs.

This is not to say that, as dogs age, they all fall apart physically and become nasty in personality. The aforementioned changes are discussed to alert owners to the things that may happen as their dogs get older. Many hardy dogs remain active and alert well into old age. However, it can be frustrating and heartbreaking for owners to see their beloved dogs change physically and temperamentally. Just know that it's the same Flat-Coated Retriever under there, and that he still loves you and appreciates your care, which he needs now more than ever.

HOW DO I CARE FOR MY AGING DOG?

Again, every dog is an individual in terms of aging. Your dog might reach the estimated "senior" age for Flat-Coats and show no signs of slowing down. However, even if he shows no outward signs of aging, he should begin a senior-care program once he reaches the determined age. He may not show it, but he's not a pup anymore! By providing him with extra attention to his veterinary care at this age, you will be practicing good preventive medicine, ensuring that the rest of your dog's life will be as long, active, happy and healthy as possible. If you do notice indications of aging, such as graying and/or changes in sleeping, eating or toileting habits, this is a sign to set up a senior-care visit with your vet right away to make sure that these changes are not related to any health problems.

To start, senior dogs should visit the vet twice yearly for exams, routine tests and overall evaluations. Many veterinarians have special screening programs especially for senior dogs that can include a thorough physical exam; blood test to determine complete blood count; serum biochemistry test, which screens for liver, kidney and blood problems as well as cancer; urinalysis; and dental exams. With these tests, it can be determined whether your dog has any health problems; the results also establish a baseline for your pet against which future test results can be compared.

In addition to these tests, your vet may suggest additional testing, including an EKG, tests for glaucoma and other problems of the eye, chest x-rays, screening for tumors, blood pressure test, test for thyroid function and screening for parasites and reassessment of his preventive program. Your vet also will ask you questions about your dog's diet and activity level, what you feed and the amounts that you feed. This information, along with his evaluation of the dog's overall condition, will enable him to suggest proper dietary changes, if needed.

This may seem like quite a work-up for your pet, but veterinarians advise that older dogs need more frequent attention so that any health problems can be detected as early as possible. Serious conditions like kidney disease, heart disease and cancer may not present outward symptoms, or the problem may go undetected if the symptoms are mistaken by owners as just part of the aging process.

There are some conditions more common in elderly dogs that

RUBDOWN REMEDY

A good remedy for an aching dog is to give him a gentle massage each day, or even a few times a day if possible. This can be especially beneficial before your dog gets out of his bed in the morning. Just as in humans, massage can decrease pain in dogs, whether the dog is arthritic or just afflicted by the stiffness that accompanies old age. Gently massage his joints and limbs, as well as petting him on his entire body. This can help his circulation and flexibility and ease any joint or muscle aches. Massaging your dog has benefits for you, too; in fact, just petting our dogs can cause reduced levels of stress and lower our blood pressure. Massage and petting also help you find any previously undetected lumps, bumps or abnormalities. Often these are not visible and only turn up by being felt.

are difficult to ignore. Cognitive dysfunction shares much in common with senility and Alzheimer's disease, and dogs are not immune. Dogs can become confused and/or disoriented, lose their house-training, have abnormal sleep-wake cycles and interact differently with their owners. Be heartened by the fact that, in some ways, there are more treatment options for dogs with cognitive dysfunction than for people with similar conditions. There is good evidence that continued stimulation in the form of games, play, training and exercise can help to maintain cognitive function. There are also medications (such as seligiline) and antioxidant-fortified senior diets that have been shown to be beneficial.

Cancer is also a condition more common in the elderly. Almost all of the cancers seen in people are also seen in pets. Even lung cancer, which is a major killer in humans, can affect pets that have regular exposure to second-hand smoke. If pets are getting regular physical examinations, cancers are often detected early. There are a variety of cancer therapies available today, and many pets continue to live happy lives with appropriate medical treatment.

Degenerative joint disease, often referred to as arthritis, is another malady common to both elderly dogs and humans. A lifetime of wear and tear on joints and running around at play eventually takes its toll and results in stiffness and difficulty in getting around. As dogs live longer and healthier lives, it is natural that they should eventually feel some of the effects of aging. Once again, if your Flat-Coat has always received regular veterinary care, he should not have been carrying extra pounds all those years and wearing those joints out before

COPING WITH A BLIND DOG

Blindness is one of the unfortunate realities of growing old, for both dogs and humans. Owners of blind dogs should not give up hope, as most dogs adapt to their compromised state with grace and patience. A sudden loss of sight poses more stress on the dog than a gradual loss, such as that through cataracts. Some dogs may need your assistance to help them get around; others will move around seemingly uninhibited. Owners may need to retrain the dog to handle some basic tasks. Teaching commands like "Wait," "Stop" and "Slow" are handy as you help the dog learn to maneuver around his world. You are now more than the team captain, you're the coach and cheerleader! If your blind dog is showing signs of depression, it is your job to encourage him and give him moral support, just as you might for a similarly affected person.

their time. If your pet was unfortunate enough to inherit hip dysplasia, osteochondrosis or any of the other developmental orthopedic diseases, battling the onset of degenerative joint disease was probably a longstanding goal. In any case, there are now many effective remedies for managing degenerative joint disease and a number of remarkable surgeries as well.

Aside from the extra veterinary care, there is much you can do at home to keep your older dog in good condition. The dog's diet is an important factor. If your dog's appetite decreases, he will not be getting the nutrients he needs. He also will lose weight, which is unhealthy for a dog at a proper weight. Conversely, an older dog's metabolism is slower and he usually exercises less, but he should not be allowed to become obese. Obesity in an older dog is especially risky, because extra pounds mean extra stress on the body, increasing his vulnerability to heart disease. Additionally, the extra pounds make it harder for the dog to move about.

You should discuss age-related feeding changes with your vet. For a dog who has lost interest in food, it may be suggested to try some different types of food until you find something new that the dog likes. For an obese dog, a "light-" formula dog food or reducing food portions may be advised, along with exercise appropriate to his physical condition and energy level.

As for exercise, the senior dog should not be allowed to become a "couch potato" despite his old age. He may not be able to handle the morning run, long walks and vigorous games of fetch, but he still needs to get up and get moving. Keep up with your daily walks, but keep the distances shorter and let your dog set the pace. If he gets to the point where he's not up for walks, let him stroll around the yard. On the other hand, many dogs remain very active in their senior years, so base changes to the exercise program on your own individual dog and what he's capable of. Don't worry, your Flat-Coated Retriever will let you know when it's time to rest.

Keep up with your grooming routine as you always have. Be extra-diligent about checking the skin and coat for problems. Older dogs can experience thinning coats

GDV IN OLDER DOGS

Bloat, or gastric dilatation-volvulus (GDV), commonly affects deep-chested dogs of all ages. Studies indicate that dogs who are over seven years of age are twice as prone to the condition as young dogs half their age. This means that you will pay extra attention to practicing bloat preventives and watching for symptoms, just as you always have with your Flat-Coat.

as a normal aging process, but they can also lose hair as a result of medical problems. Some thinning is normal, but patches of baldness or the loss of significant amounts of hair is not.

Hopefully, you've been regular with brushing your dog's teeth throughout his life. Healthy teeth directly affect overall good health. We already know that bacteria from gum infections can enter the dog's body through the damaged gums and travel to the organs. At a stage in life when his organs don't function as well as they used to, you don't want anything to put additional strain on them. Clean teeth also contribute to a healthy immune system. Offering the dental-type chews in addition to toothbrushing can help, as they remove plaque and tartar as the dog chews.

Along with the same good care you've given him all of his life, pay a little extra attention to your dog in his senior years and keep up with twice-yearly trips to the vet. The sooner a problem is uncovered, the greater the chances of a full recovery.

SAYING GOODBYE

While you can help your dog live as long a life as possible, you can't help him live forever. A dog's lifespan is short when compared to that of a human, so it is inevitable that pet owners will experience loss. To many, losing a beloved dog is like losing a family member. Our dogs are part of our lives every day; they are our true loyal friends and always seem to know when it's time to comfort us, to celebrate with us or to just provide the company of a caring friend. Even whether we know that our dog is nearing his final days, we can never quite prepare for his being gone.

When the end comes for a beloved pet, it is a very difficult time for owners, especially if they are faced with making a choice regarding euthanasia, more commonly known as having a dog "put to sleep" or "put down." Euthanasia can be defined as the act of ending the life of an individual suffering from a terminal illness or incurable condition.

Veterinary euthanasia means that a pet is injected with a concentrated dose of anesthesia, causing unconsciousness within a few seconds and death soon after. This process is painless for the dog; the only discomfort he may feel is the prick of the needle, the same as he would with any other injection.

The decision of whether or not to euthanize is undoubtedly the hardest that owners have to make regarding their pets. It is a very emotional decision, yet it requires much clear thinking and discussion with the vet and, of course, all family members. Owners may also seek religious advice. During this time, owners will experience many different feelings: guilt, sadness, possibly anger at over having to make this type of decision. Many times, it is hard to actually come to a decision, thinking that maybe the dog will miraculously recover or that maybe he will succumb to his illness, making the decision no longer necessary.

You have many factors to consider. Of course, you will speak with your vet and will involve all members of the family in each step of the decision-making process. Some of the things to think about include the current quality of your pet's life, whether he is constantly ill and/or in pain, whether there are things you can do to give him a comfortable life even if he has an incurable condition, whether you've explored all treatment problems, whether you've discussed the behavioral aspects of your pet's problems with an expert and whether you've thoroughly discussed with the vet your dog's prognosis and the likelihood of his being able to function and enjoy life.

Of course, the aforementioned considerations present just some of the things that you will need to think about. You will have many questions and concerns of your own. Never feel pressured; take time to make a decision with which you will be comfortable.

MEMORIALIZING YOUR PET

Whether and how you choose to memorialize your pet is completely up to you. Some owners feel that this helps their healing process by allowing them some closure. Likewise, some owners feel that memorialization is a meaningful way to acknowledge their departed pets. Some owners opt to bury their deceased pets in their own yards, using special stones, flowers or trees to mark the sites. Others opt for the services of a pet cemetery, in which many of the privileges available for humans, such as funeral and viewing services, caskets and gravestones, are available for pets. Cremation is an option, either individual or communal. Owners then can opt to have their dogs' ashes buried, scattered or kept in an urn as a memorial. Your vet will likely know of the services available in your locality and can help you make arrangements if you choose one of these options.

SHOWING YOUR

FLAT-COATED RETRIEVER

CONFORMATION SHOWING

Is dog showing in your blood? Are you excited by the idea of gaiting your handsome Flat-Coated Retriever around the ring to the thunderous applause of an enthusiastic audience? Are you certain that your beloved Flat-Coated Retriever is flawless? You are not alone! Every loving owner thinks that his dog has no faults, or too few to mention. No matter how many times an owner reads the breed standard, he cannot find any faults in his aristocratic companion dog. If this sounds like you, and if you are considering entering your Flat-Coated Retriever in a dog show, here are some basic questions to ask yourself:

- Did you purchase a "show-quality" puppy from the breeder?
- Is your puppy at least six months of age?
- Does the puppy exhibit correct show type for his breed?
- Does your puppy have any disqualifying faults?
- Is your Flat-Coated Retriever registered with the American Kennel Club?
- How much time do you have to devote to training, grooming, conditioning and exhibiting your dog?
- Do you understand the rules and regulations of a dog show?
- Do you have time to learn how to show your dog properly?
- Do you have the financial resources to invest in showing your dog?

MEET THE AKC

The American Kennel Club is the main governing body of the dog sport in the United States. Founded in 1884, the AKC consists of 500 or more independent dog clubs plus 4,500 affiliated clubs, all of which follow the AKC rules and regulations. Additionally, the AKC maintains a registry for pure-bred dogs in the US and works to preserve the integrity of the sport and its continuation in the country. Over 1,000,000 dogs are registered each year, representing about 150 recognized breeds. There are over 15,000 competitive events held annually for which over 2,000,000 dogs enter to participate. Dogs compete to earn over 40 different titles, from Champion to Companion Dog to Master Agility Champion.

- Will you show the dog yourself or hire a professional handler?
- Do you have a vehicle that can accommodate your weekend trips to the dog shows?

Success in the show ring requires more than a pretty face, a waggy tail and a pocketful of liver. Even though dog shows can be exciting and enjoyable, the sport of conformation makes great demands on the exhibitors and the dogs. Winning exhibitors live for their dogs, devoting time and money to their dogs' presentation, conditioning and training. Very few novices, even those with good dogs, will find themselves in the winners' circle, though it does happen. Don't be disheartened, though. Every exhibitor began as a novice and worked his way up to the Group ring. It's the "working your way up" part that you must keep in mind.

Assuming that you have purchased a puppy of the correct type and quality for showing, let's begin to examine the world of showing and what's required to get started. Although the entry fee into a dog show is nominal, there are lots of other hidden costs involved with "finishing" your Flat-Coated Retriever, that is, making him a champion. Things like equipment, travel, training and conditioning all cost money. A more serious campaign will include fees for a professional handler, boarding, cross-country travel and advertising. Top-winning show dogs can represent a very considerable investment—over $100,000 has been spent in campaigning some dogs. (The investment can be less, of course, for owners who don't use professional handlers.)

Many owners, on the other hand, enter their "average" Flat-Coated Retrievers in dog shows for the fun and enjoyment of it. Dog showing makes an absorbing hobby, with many rewards for dogs and owners alike. If you're having fun, meeting other people who share your interests and enjoying the overall experience, you likely will catch the "bug." Once the dog-show bug bites, its effects can last a lifetime; it's certainly much better than a deer tick! Soon you will be envisioning

BECOMING A CHAMPION

An official AKC championship of record requires that a dog accumulate 15 points under three different judges, including two "majors" under different judges. Points are awarded based on the number of dogs entered into competition, varying from breed to breed and place to place. A win of three, four or five points is considered a "major." The AKC annually assigns a schedule of points to adjust to the variations that accompany a breed's popularity and the population of a given area.

yourself in the center ring at the Westminster Kennel Club Dog Show in New York City, competing for the prestigious Best in Show cup. This magical dog show is televised annually from Madison Square Garden, and the victorious dog becomes a celebrity overnight.

Visiting a dog show as a spectator is a great place to start learning. Pick up the show catalog to find out what time your breed is being shown, who is judging the breed and in which ring the classes will be held. To start, Flat-Coated Retrievers compete against other Flat-Coated Retrievers, and the winner is selected as Best of Breed by the judge. This is the procedure for each breed. At a group show, all of the Best of

The time and training required for the show ring build a bond between dog and handler. You can learn to show your own dog, an experience that will be fun and rewarding for both of you.

AKC GROUPS

For showing purposes, the American Kennel Club divides its recognized breeds into seven groups: Sporting Dogs, Hounds, Working Dogs, Terriers, Toys, Non-Sporting Dogs and Herding Dogs. The Flat-Coated Retriever is in the Sporting Group.

FIVE CLASSES AT SHOWS

At most AKC all-breed shows, there are five regular classes offered: Puppy, Novice, Bred-by-Exhibitor, American-bred and Open. The Puppy Class is usually divided as 6 to 9 months of age and 9 to 12 months of age. When deciding in which class to enter your dog, whether male or female, you must carefully check the show schedule to make sure that you have selected the right class. Depending on the age of the dog, previous first-place wins and the sex of the dog, you must make the best choice. It is possible to enter a one-year-old dog who has not won sufficient first places in any of the non-Puppy Classes, though the competition is more intense the further you progress from the Puppy Class.

Breed winners go on to compete for Group One in their respective groups. For example, all Best of Breed winners in a given group compete against each other; this is done for all seven groups. Finally, all seven group winners go head to head in the ring for the Best in Show award.

What most spectators don't understand is the basic idea of conformation. A dog show is often referred as a "conformation" show. This means that the judge should decide how each dog stacks up (conforms) to the breed standard for his given breed: how well does this Flat-Coated Retriever conform to the ideal representative detailed in the standard? Ideally, this is what happens. In reality, however, this ideal often gets slighted as the judge compares Flat-Coated Retriever #1 to Flat-Coated Retriever #2. Again, the ideal is that each dog is judged based on his merits in comparison to his breed standard, not in comparison to the other dogs in the ring. It is easier for judges to compare dogs of the same breed to decide which they think is the better specimen; in the Group and Best in Show ring, however, it is very difficult to compare one breed to another, like apples to oranges. Thus the dog's conformation to the breed standard—not to mention advertising dollars and good handling—is essential to success in conformation shows. The dog described in the standard (the standard for each AKC breed is written and approved by the breed's national parent club and then submitted to the AKC for approval) is the perfect dog of that breed, and breeders keep their eye on the standard when they choose which dogs to breed, hoping to get closer and closer to that elusive ideal with each litter.

Another good first step for the novice is to join a dog club. You will be astonished by the many and different kinds of dog clubs in the country, with about 5,000 clubs holding events every year. Most clubs require that prospective new members present two letters of recommendation from existing members. Perhaps you've made some friends visiting a show held by a particular club and you would like to join that club. Dog clubs may specialize in a single breed, like a local or regional Flat-Coated Retriever club, or in a specific pursuit, such as obedience, tracking or hunting tests. There are all-breed clubs for all dog enthusiasts; they may sponsor special training days, seminars on topics like grooming or handling or lectures on breeding or canine genetics. There are also clubs that specialize in certain types of dogs, like hunting dogs, herding dogs, companion dogs, etc.

A parent club is the national organization, sanctioned by the AKC, which promotes and safeguards its breed in the country. The Flat-Coated Retriever Society of America was formed in 1960 and can be found on the Internet at www.fcrsainc.org. The parent club holds an annual national specialty show, usually in a different city each year, in which many of the country's top dogs, handlers and breeders gather to compete. At a specialty show, only members of a single breed are invited to participate. There are also group specialties, in which all members of a group are invited. For more information about dog clubs in your area, contact the AKC at www.akc.org on the Internet or write them at their Raleigh, NC address.

OBEDIENCE TRIALS

Mrs. Helen Whitehouse Walker, a Standard Poodle fancier, can be credited with introducing obedience trials to the United States in the 1930s. Now more than 2,000 trials each year attract over 100,000 dogs and their owners. Any dog registered with the AKC, regardless of neutering or other disqualifications that would preclude entry in conformation competition, can participate in obedience trials.

There are three levels of difficulty in obedience competition. The first (and easiest) level is

FOUL!

The sport of conformation is governed by many rules for handlers, dogs and spectators. A judge may dismiss an entry from the ring for "double handling" if the judge rightly believes that a spectator is intentionally interfering with the proceedings to benefit a particular dog. The boisterous (and, sometimes, manipulative) spectator who purposefully is distracting, cajoling or exciting a dog can also be removed from ringside or expelled by the show committee for double handling.

the Novice, in which dogs can earn the Companion Dog (CD) title. The intermediate level is the Open level, in which the Companion Dog Excellent (CDX) title is awarded. The advanced level is the Utility level, in which dogs compete for the Utility Dog (UD) title. Classes at each level are further divided into "A" and "B," with "A" for beginners and "B" for those with more experience. In order to win a title at a given level, a dog must earn three "legs." A "leg" is accomplished when a dog scores 170 or higher (200 is a perfect score). The scoring system gets a little trickier when you understand that a dog must score more than 50% of the points available for each exercise in order to actually earn the points. Available points for each exercise range between 20 and 40.

Once he's earned the UD title, a dog can go on to win the prestigious title of Utility Dog Excellent (UDX) by winning "legs" in ten shows. Additionally, Utility Dogs who win "legs" in Open B and Utility B earn points toward the lofty title of Obedience Trial Champion (OTCh.). Established in 1977 by the AKC, this title requires a dog to earn 100 points as well as three first places in a combination of Open B and Utility B classes under three different judges. The "brass ring" of obedience competition is the AKC's National Obedience Invitational. This is an exclusive competition for only the cream of the obedience crop. In order to qualify for the invitational, a dog must be ranked in either the top 25 all-breeds in obedience or in the top three for his breed in obedience. The title at stake here is that of National Obedience Champion (NOC).

AGILITY TRIALS

Agility trials became sanctioned by the AKC in August 1994, when the first licensed agility trials were held. Since that time, agility certainly has grown in popularity by leaps and bounds, literally! The AKC allows all registered breeds (including Miscellaneous Class breeds) to participate, providing the dog is 12 months of age or older. Agility is designed so that the handler demonstrates how well the dog can work at his side. The handler directs his dog through, over, under and around an obstacle course that includes jumps, tires, the dog walk, weave poles, pipe tunnels, collapsed tunnels and more. While working his way through the course, the dog must keep one eye and ear on the handler and the rest of his body on the course. The handler runs along with the dog, giving verbal and hand signals to guide the dog through the course.

The first organization to promote agility trials in the US was the United States Dog Agility

Association, Inc. (USDAA). Established in 1986, the USDAA sparked the formation of many member clubs around the country. To participate in USDAA trials, dogs must be at least 18 months of age. The USDAA and AKC both offer titles to winning dogs, although the exercises and requirements of the two organizations differ.

Agility trials are a great way to keep your dog active, and they will keep you running, too! You should join a local agility club to learn more about the sport. These clubs offer sessions in which you can introduce your dog to the various obstacles as well as training classes to prepare him for competition. In no time, your dog will be climbing A-frames, crossing the dog walk and flying over hurdles, all with you right beside him. Your heart will leap every time your dog jumps through the hoop—and you'll be having just as much (if not more) fun!

TRACKING

Tracking tests are exciting ways to test your Flat-Coated Retriever's instinctive scenting ability on a competitive level. All dogs have a nose, and all breeds are welcome in tracking tests. The first AKC-licensed tracking test took place in 1937 as part of the Utility level at an obedience trial, and thus competitive tracking was officially begun. The first title, Tracking Dog (TD), was offered in 1947, ten years after the first official tracking test. It was not until 1980 that the AKC added the title Tracking Dog Excellent (TDX), which was followed by the title Versatile Surface Tracking (VST) in 1995. Champion Tracker (CT) is awarded to a dog who has earned all three of those titles.

The TD level is the first and most basic level in tracking, progressing in difficulty to the TDX and then the VST. A dog must follow a track laid by a human 30 to 120 minutes prior in order to earn the TD title. The track is about 500 yards long and contains up to 5 directional

Dog shows are enjoyable events where you can meet people with the same interests as your own and where you can get friendly advice about many aspects of dogdom.

changes. At the next level, the TDX, the dog must follow a 3- to 5-hour-old track over a course that is up to 1,000 yards long and has up to 7 directional changes. In the most difficult level, the VST, the track is up to 5 hours old and located in an urban setting.

FIELD TRIALS

Field trials are offered to the retrievers, pointers and spaniel breeds of the Sporting Group as well as to the Beagles, Dachshunds and Bassets of the Hound Group. The purpose of field trials is to demonstrate a dog's ability to perform his breed's original purpose in the field. The events vary depending on the type of dog, but in all trials dogs compete against one another for placement and for points toward their Field Champion (FC) titles. Flat-Coats that earn their FC titles plus their championship in the show ring are known as Dual Champions; this is extremely prestigious, as it shows that the dog is the ideal blend of form and function, excelling in both areas.

Retriever field trials, designed to simulate "an ordinary day's shoot," are popular and likely the most demanding of these trials. Dogs must "mark" the location of downed feathered game and then return the birds to the shooter. Successful dogs are able to "mark" the downed game by remembering where the bird fell as well as by correct use of the wind and terrain. Dogs are tested both on land and in water.

Difficulty levels are based on the number of birds downed as well as the number of "blind retrieves" (where a bird is placed away from the view of the dog and the handler directs the dog by the use of hand signals and verbal commands). The term "Non-Slip" retriever, often applied to these trials, refers to a dog that is steady at the handler's side until commanded to go. Every field trial includes four stakes of increasing levels of difficulty. Each stake is judged by a team of two judges who look for many natural abilities, including steadiness, courage, style and control, as well as training.

FOR MORE INFORMATION....

For reliable up-to-date information about registration, dog shows and other canine competitions, contact one of the national registries by mail or via the Internet.

American Kennel Club
5580 Centerview Dr., Raleigh, NC 27606-3390
www.akc.org

United Kennel Club
100 E. Kilgore Road, Kalamazoo, MI 49002
www.ukcdogs.com

Canadian Kennel Club
89 Skyway Ave., Suite 100, Etobicoke, Ontario
M9W 6R4 Canada
www.ckc.ca

HUNTING TESTS

Hunting tests are not competitive like field trials, and participating dogs are judged against a standard, as in a conformation show. The first hunting tests were devised by the North American Hunting Retriever Association (NAHRA) as an alternative to field trials for retriever owners to appreciate their dogs' innate ability in the field without the expense and pressure of a formal field trial. The intent of hunting tests is the same as that of field trials: to test the dog's ability in a simulated hunting scenario.

The AKC instituted its hunting tests in June 1985; since then, their popularity has grown tremendously. The AKC offers three titles at hunting tests, Junior Hunter (JH), Senior Hunter (SH) and Master Hunter (MH). Each title requires that the dog earn qualifying "legs" at the tests: the JH requiring four; the SH, five; and the MH, six. In addition to the AKC, the United Kennel Club also offers hunting tests through its affiliate club, the Hunting Retriever Club, Inc. (HRC), which began the tests in 1984. This can be a rewarding pursuit for interested Flat-Coat owners.

If you have the time and a large enough yard, you can set up your own training course at home.

INDEX

*Page numbers in **boldface** indicate illustrations.*

Activities 22-23, 95-96
—senior dog 144
Adenovirus 109
Adult
—adoption 74
—feeding 59
—health 103
—training 72, 75
Age 77
Aggression 51, 75, 86, 110
Agility 22, 96
—trials 152
Aging 103, 140
All-Aged Field Trial Stake 16
All-Aged Stake 15
Alpha role 84
American Heartworm Society 129
American Kennel Club 147, 151, 154, 155
—breed standard 24-29
—Companion Animal Recovery 70
—registration 16
Ancylostoma caninum **125, 128**
Annual vet exams 103
Antifreeze 46, 47, 107
Appetite loss 57, 103, 107
Arthritis 142, 143
Ascarid **124**, 125
Ascaris lumbricoides **124**
Assistance dogs 22
Atherbram Kennel 15
Atherbram Stella 16
Attention 85, 87, 92
Backpacking 96
Bathing 64
Bedding 39, 50, 80
Behavior
—senior dog 140
Best in Show 150
Best of Breed 149
Black Queen 14
Black Quilt 14
Blindness 143
Bloat 59, 62, 104, 105, 107, 144
Boarding 70-71
Body language 75, 82, 89
Body temperature 101
Bones 40
Bordetella *109*
Bordetella bronchiseptica 110
Boredom 19, 63
Borrelia burgdorferi 109
Borreliosis 110
Bowls 37
Bramcroft Dandy 16
Bramcroft Obedience Trophy 16
Breed club 31
Breed name 10
Breed standard 150
Breeder 31-36, 99, 150
Brushing 63
Buccleuch Kennel 11
Burial 146
Canadian Kennel Club 154
Cancer 110, 114, 138, 143
Canine cough 109
Canine development schedule 77
Car travel 49, 71, 86
Cat 50, 86
Cataracts 134
Champion 148
Champion Tracker 153
Chemicals 47
Cherry eye 132
Chew toys 39-42, 55, 79-80
Chewing 39, 54-55, 86
Cheyletiella mite **121**
Chiggers 123
Children 20, 49, 51, 54-55, 56, 75, 84, 86
Chocolate 46, 60
Classes at shows 150
Clicker training 91
Clubs 150
Coat 15, 20
—senior dog 144
Cognitive dysfunction 105-106, 140, 143
Cold weather 141
Collar 42-44, 71, 86
Collie eye 135
Color 10, 11
Come 86, 90, 92
Command 87
—potty 80
—practicing 88, 91
Commitment of ownership 34, 36
Companion Dog 151
Companion Dog Excellent 152
Companionship 18
Conformation 148-151
Conjunctiva 131
Conjunctivitis 131
Consistency 52, 56, 57, 85, 87
—for the older dog 140
Cooke, H. Reginald 12-14
Core vaccines 110
Corneal disease 132-133
Cornwall-Leigh, Colonel 12-13
Coronavirus 109, 110
Correction 85
Cox, Mr. Harding 12, 13
Crate 37-39, 49-50, 79
—pads 39
—training 75-83
Cremation 146
Crying 50, 80
Ctenocephalides canis **116**
Curly-Coated Retriever 10
Dangers in the home 44, 47
Death of pet 145-146
DEET 123
Degenerative joint disease 143
Demodex mite **123**
Demodicosis 122-123
Dental care 101, 103, 107
—of senior dog 145
Dental problems 57, 103
Depression 143
Destructive behavior 19, 63
Diet
—adult 59-60
—puppy 57-59
—senior 60, 144
Dilatation 144
Dipylidium caninum 126 **128**
Dirofilaria immitis 127, **128, 129**
Discipline 54, 83-84
Distemper 16, 109, 110
Distichiasis 131
DOC 15-16
Dog club 31, 151
Dog flea 116
Dog-fight 86
Dominance 88
Double handling 151
Down 56, 81, 88-89
Downing, Homer 15-16
Down/stay 91
Drop it 84
Drug detection 23
Dry baths 64
Dry eye syndrome 131
Dual Champion 154
Dual-purpose dogs 11, 13, 15, 16-17
Ear
—cleaning 67
—mite infestation 67, 121-122
Echinococcus multilocularis 127
Ectopic cilia 131
Ectropion 130
Elbow dysplasia 114
Emergency care 107, 136-137
Entropion 130
Epilepsy 114
Estrus 110
Ethylene glycol 44
Ettington prefix 11
Euthanasia 145-146
Exercise 18, 62-63
—pen 78
—senior dog 144
Expenses of ownership 38
External parasites 116-123
Eye disease 130-135
Eyelash abnormalities 131
Family meeting the puppy 48-49
Fear period 52
Feeding 57-62
Fenced yard 44, 86
Fertilizer 47
Field Champion 154
Field Trial Trophy 16
Field trials 22, 96, 154
Finding lost dog 70
First aid 107, 136-137
First night in new home 49
Flat-Coated Retriever Association 15
Flat-Coated Retriever Society of America 16
Fleas **116**, 117, **118**
Food 79
—bowls 37
—lack of interest in 57, 103, 107
—rewards 73, 85, 94
—toxic to dogs 46, 60
Gastric torsion 59, 62, 104, 105, 107, 144
Genetic testing 99
Getting started in showing 149
Giardia 109
Give it 84
Glaucoma 133-134
Go-to-ground events 95
Golden Retriever 10, 14
Grapes 60
Greenfield June 15
Grooming 20, 68
Group competition 150
Grouse of Riverside 13
Growth 58, 59
Guide dogs 22
Gum disease 103
Handler 148
Health 47
—adult 103
—breed-specific concerns 112-114
—insurance for pets 108
—journal 48
—puppy 32, 48, 99
—senior dog 105, 142
Heart disease 105
Heartworm 101, 127, **128, 129**
Heat cycle 110
Heat-related problems 70, 141
Heel 93-94
Hepatitis 109, 110
Herding trials 95
Hereditary problems 112-114
Heterodoxus spiniger **122**
High Leigh Blarney 13, **14**
Hiking 96
Hip dysplasia 112-114, 144
HomeAgain™ Companion Animal Retrieval System 69
Homemade toys 42
Hookworm **125, 128**
Hot weather 141
House rules 74
House-training 37, 39, 43, 75-83
Hunting 9-10, 22, 95
—events 96, 155
—Retriever Club 155
Hypothyroidism 114
Identification 68-70
Infectious diseases 108-111
Insurance 108

Internal parasites 124-129
Ixodes dammini **119-120**
Jet 16
Jumping up 56, 81
Junior Hunter 155
Kennel Club, The 11, 15, 32
Keratoconjunctivitis sicca 131
Kidney problems 105
Labrador Retriever 10, 11, 14
Leash 44-46, 82, 86
—pulling on 94
Leave it 86
Lens dislocation 134
Lens luxation 135
Leptospirosis 109, 110
Lethargy 107
Lid conformational abnormalities 130
Lifespan 60, 103, 139
Litter box 50
Liver 11
Lost dog 70
Louse **122**
Lumps and bumps 107, 114, 138
Lure-coursing 95
Lyme disease 109, 110
Malmesbury Kennel 11
Mammary cancer 110
Massage 142
Master Hunter 155
Maturity 20, 22, 58
Memorialization 145
Methods of training 75
Microchip 69
Miscellaneous Class 152
Mites **121**, 122, **123**
Mosquitoes 123, 127, 129
Mounting 110
Music 11
Nail clipping 65
Name 87, 93
National Obedience Champion 152
Neutering 48, 101, 110-111
Nipping 54-55
Non-core vaccines 110
North American Hunting Retriever Association 155
Norway 23
Nose 22
Nuts 60
O'Neill, Stanley 15
Obedience 22, 89
—Classes 95
—Trial Champion 152
—trials 95, 151
Obesity 59-61, 144
Off 56, 81
Okay 89-90, 94
Onions 60
Optic neuritis 135
Oral instincts 19
Orthopedic Foundation for Animals 112, 114
Orthopedic problems 112-114
—senior dog 143
Osteochondrosis dissecans 144
Other dogs 110
Other pets 50, 75
Otodectes cynotis 121
Outdoor safety 47
Ovariohysterectomy 111
Ownership 34-37
—expenses of 38
—qualifications 30
Pack animals 52, 73, 83
Pain 107
Paper-training 76, 82
Parainfluenza 109, 110
Parasites 37
—control 101
—external 116-123
—internal 124-129
Parent club 151
Parvovirus 109, 110
Patellar luxation 112
Patience 74, 85
Pedigree 35, 36
Personality 18-22
Pewcroft Kennel 15
Pewcroft Prefect 15-16
Phizacklea, Mr. 15
Plants 47, 107
Playtime 84, 92
Poisons 46-47, 60, 107
Popularity 14-15, 16
Positive reinforcement 21, 44, 49, 84, 88, 91
Practicing 91
—commands 88
Praise 73, 84-85, 95
Preventive care 99-106
Proglottid **127**
Prolapsed gland 132
Prostate problems 110
Pulling on leash 94
Punishment 83-85
Puppy
—common problems 54
—diet 57
—establishing leadership 73
—exercise 63
—feeding 57
—first car ride 49
—first night home 49
—growth 58
—health 32, 48, 99, 101
—kindergarten training 87
—meeting the family 48, 49
—needs 76
—parasites 37
—personality 35, 101
—selection 31-37, 99
—show quality 147-148
—socialization 50
—teething 55
—training 53, 72, 85
Puppy-proofing 43, 47
Rabies 109, 110
Racing 95
Raisins 60
Rawhide 40
Redesdale, Lord 14
Registration
—AKC 16
—certificate 35
Retinal disease 134-135
Retrievers 9
Retriever field trials 154
Rewards 73, 83, 84-85, 94
—food 84
Rhabditis **128**
Riverside Kennel 12
Roaming 110
Rope toys 41
Roundworm 37, **124**, 125, **128**
Safety 38, 44, 46-47, 54, 60, 78-80, 86, 92
—for the older dog 139
—in the car 71, 86
—outdoors 47
—with toys 40-42
Safety commands 86
Sarcoptes scabiei **121**
SARD 135
Scabies 121
Scent attraction 82
Schedule 78
Scotch collies 11
Search and rescue 23
Senior dog
—behavioral changes 140
—consistency 140
—dental care 145
—diet 60, 144
—exercise 144
—health 103
—safety 139
—signs of aging 140
—veterinary care 105-106, 141-145
Senior Hunter 155
Service dog 22
Shirley, Sewallis Evelyn 11, 12
Shotgun 9
Shows
—costs of 148
—quality 147-148
Sit 87
Sit/stay 90
Skin 107
Socialization 51-53, 75, 87, 101
Soft/squeaky toys 41
Spaying 48, 101, 110-111
Specialty show 151
Sporting dogs 95
Spot bath 64
St. John's Water Dogs 10-11
Standard 24, 150
Stay 90
Stray dog 71
Stress 95
Supervision 54-55, 81
Surgery 111
Sweets 44
Swimming 22, 62, 68
Taenia pisiformis **127**
Tapeworm 126, **127, 128**
Tattoo 70
Teeth 101, 103, 107
Teething period 55
Temperament 18-22, 33
—evaluation 101
Temperature
—taking your dog's 101
Testicular cancer 110
Therapy Dog 96
Third eyelid
—prolapse of the gland 132
Thyroid 114
Tick-borne diseases 119
Ticks 109, **119-120**
Timing 82, 85, 92
Toby of Riverside 13
Toxascaris leonine 124
Toxins 46-47, 60, 107
Toxocara canis **124**
Toys 39-42, 55, 79-80, 84
Tracheobronchitis 109
Tracking 22, 96, 153
—Dog 153
—Dog Excellent 153
Training 20-22
—basic principles of 72, 85
—clicker 91
—commands 87
—consistency in 52, 56, 87
—crate 39, 75-83
—early 53
—getting started 86
—importance of timing 82, 92
—proper attitude 20, 75
—puppy 85
—tips 22, 44, 54
Trash can 54
Traveling 38, 49, 71, 86
Treats 49, 59, 73, 84-85
—weaning off in training 94
Trichuris sp. **126**
Tricks 96
Type 147-148
United Kennel Club 154, 155
United States Dog Agility Association 152
Urine marking 110
Utility Dog 152
—Excellent 152
Utility Dog Tracker 15
Uveitis 133
Vaccinations 48, 52, 101, 108-111
Versatile Surface Tracking 153
Veterinarian 31, 40-41, 47-48, 86, 101, 103, 106-108
Veterinary insurance 108
Veterinary specialties 107
Visiting the litter 33-35
Volvulus 144
Wait 86
Walker, Mrs. Helen Whitehouse 151
Watchdogs 20
Water 61, 62, 79
—bowls 37
Wavy-Coated Retriever 10-11
Weather 141
Weight 59-61
West Nile virus 123
Westminster Kennel Club 149
Whining 50, 80
Whipworm **126**
World Wars 15
Worm control 126
Worming treatment 37
Wyndham 11
Yard 47
Yellow color 10

My Flat-Coated Retriever

PUT YOUR PUPPY'S FIRST PICTURE HERE

Dog's Name ______________________________

Date ______________ Photographer ______________________